Mary Eastwood

Antique
Scientific Instruments

Gerard L'E Turner

Antique Scientific Instruments

BLANDFORD PRESS

Poole   Dorset

First published in the U.K. 1980

Copyright © 1980 Blandford Press Ltd.,
Link House, West Street,
Poole, Dorset, BH15 1LL

**British Library Cataloguing in
Publication Data**
Turner, Gerard L'Estrange
 Antique scientific instruments.
 1. Scientific apparatus and instruments –
 Collectors and collecting
 I. Title
 681'.75'09   Q185

ISBN 0 7137 0923 5 (Hardback edition)
ISBN 0 7137 1068 3 (Paperback edition)

Phototypeset in Monophoto Apollo
by Oliver Burridge and Co. Ltd.

Printed in Hong Kong
by South China Printing Co.

Contents

Acknowledgements

The author wishes to thank the curators of many collections all over the world for their kind co-operation over a number of years.

Instruments in the colour photographs have been reproduced by kind permission of the following: Birmingham City Museum: 66; City of Dundee Museums and Art Galleries Department: 12; Director of the Royal Scottish Museum, Edinburgh, (Crown copyright): 34; Kodak Museum, Harrow: 43, 44; Maritime Museum, Poole: 19; Musées Royaux d'Art et d'Histoire, Brussels: 9; Museo di Storia della Scienza, Florence: 1, 55; Museum of the History of Science, Oxford: 2, 3, 5, 7, 21, 25, 30, 31, 37, 39, 40, 42, 65, 69; Norfolk Museums Service (Bridewell Museum): 36; Private Collections: 28, 29, 33, 38, 41, 59, 63, 64; Royal Swedish Academy of Sciences, Stockholm: 24, 49; Science Museum, London: 22, 48, 50, 54, 56, 57, 60, 68; Snowshill Manor, Worcestershire, (a property of the National Trust), photographed by Robin Fletcher: 4, 8, 10, 11, 13, 14, 15, 17, 20, 23, 26, 35, 51, 58, 61, 62, 63, 64, 67; Teyler's Museum, Haarlem: 16, 47; Whipple Museum of the History of Science, Cambridge: 6, 18, 32; Utrecht Universiteits Museum: 27, 45, 46, 52, 53.

Black and white illustrations are reproduced by courtesy of the following: Copyright Bodleian Library, Oxford (page 32); Trustees of the British Museum (page 151); Copyright Kodak Museum (page 123); Crown copyright, Science Museum, London (pages 37, 46, 126–127, 140).

Introduction

The impulse to collect is an almost universal one, certainly among settled and civilised communities. It satisfies the hunting and acquisitive instincts, the love of beauty, intellectual curiosity; it can also make economic sense. Fine art objects are the prime targets for collectors, with hand-crafted products running a close second. People have collected paintings and sculpture, porcelain, metalware, furniture and textiles for centuries. With the voyages of discovery in the sixteenth century came the vogue for collecting 'rarities' which included objects of natural history such as fossils, archaeological specimens, and ethnographic artefacts from unfamiliar cultures.

Scientific instruments began to be produced in significant numbers only from the seventeenth century onwards, but it was not long before these too became collectors' items. They are in a different category from those already mentioned, in that although they may be masterpieces of craftsmanship and beautifully embellished, their function is of greater importance than their appearance. They were intended for use, not decoration. They appeal first to the mind, and give a measure of the intellectual achievement of the age in which they were made. They are ideas made into brass, ivory or wood.

In the twentieth century, we have all come to accept a vast range of technical, often very complex, equipment for use in our everyday lives. Science for the ordinary man has passed through the stage of something to marvel at, and has become the very substance of his life style. In the Western world, this process has taken roughly three centuries. Some instruments survive from the beginning of this period, the mid-seventeenth century; a few, indeed, from much earlier, but these are of great value because of their age, and are to be found only in museums and private collections. The vast majority of antique instruments available today to the collector date from the Victorian and Edwardian periods.

Scientific instruments were divided by the makers themselves into three broad categories, and it is useful to be aware of these when studying such artefacts today. Dudley Adams, for example, a member of one of the best-known firms of the eighteenth century, described himself as a 'Mathematical, Optical and Philosophical Instrument Maker'. This signified that he made or retailed the full range of scientific apparatus. Other makers, such as John Cuff and James Short, were specialists. Short described himself as producing 'solely reflecting telescopes'.

Mathematical instruments were the earliest to be made, and were so called because their purpose was to make measurements, and because a mathematical principle was embodied in their construction. Making a sundial presents a trigonometrical problem, and its purpose is to measure and record the passing of time, one of man's most basic needs. Instruments of measurement were developed first to plot out the progress of the seasons and the day for agricultural purposes, and then to aid travel by land and sea. The astrolabe was an omnibus instrument, which told the time, and also made possible angular measurement for astronomical and surveying purposes. All physical measurement basically reduces itself into measuring time, length and mass. Other mathematical instruments include the quadrant for measuring elevation, the theodolite for surveying, and a wide variety of rules, graduated scales and measures for weight and volume. The makers of these instruments were skilled engravers, and many learnt their trade from the map-makers of the Low Countries.

The properties of mirrors were known from classical times, and spectacles were in use in the Middle Ages, and so it is odd that optical instruments were late to develop. The combining of two lenses together was not seriously attempted until the very beginning of the seventeenth century, when several possible inventors vied for priority. One reason for the late development was undoubtedly the poor quality of glass available, which inhibited the optical performance of both telescopes and microscopes until the nineteenth century. For this reason the finest telescopes of the eighteenth century had their optics made not of glass but of polished metal. Nevertheless, optical instruments, introducing man for the first time to the new worlds of the very distant and the very small, had a tremendous impact on the popular imagination.

This impact, indeed, could be said to have stimulated the market for the third category of scientific instruments: philosophical instruments. These were pieces of apparatus designed to produce and demonstrate various physical effects. The two most ubiquitous and popular were the air pump and the frictional electrical machine. The air pump, designed to create a vacuum, was the invention of Robert Hooke, when he was assistant to Robert Boyle in his research on gases. Controversy raged throughout the eighteenth century on the nature of electricity, and electrical machines were used both by serious scientists and for spectacular popular demonstrations. Electricity was believed also to have a therapeutic effect, and John Wesley believed it to be a heaven-sent source of cheap medical treatment for the poor. There were many other demonstration pieces of apparatus, designed to show the effects of magnetism, heat, gravity, friction and so on. These instruments continued to be produced for teaching purposes throughout the eighteenth and nineteenth centuries, and into the present century. Many are still to be found hidden in school laboratory cupboards. Some, indeed, have found a new and exciting lease of life as playthings. They are intriguing, attractive to look at, and of interest both to the historian and the scientist.

These three categories have been retained in the following chapters of this book, though the broad group of mathematical instruments has been subdivided into five more compact sections: astronomy and time-telling, navigation instruments, surveying instruments, drawing and calculating instruments, and weights and measures. A chapter has also been included on medical instruments, which, though made by cutlers rather than scientific instrument makers, are still a variety of scientific apparatus.

1
Astronomy and Time-Telling

Astronomy, the systematic study of the heavens, is important for time-telling by day and night, for guidance in travel by sea and land, and also for keeping a record of the progress of the seasons. This last function became important when settlements were formed and the requirements of agriculture demanded a calendar in order to record the annual cycle: lambing must be arranged to occur when new grass is available in the spring; seed must be sown at a time when the earth will be warm enough to germinate it. Astronomy is therefore one of the earliest sciences, and its practitioners used crude instruments and methods of computation.

Some of the earliest observatories known are monumental in scale, using natural features allied with stone obelisks as foresights and backsights. Examples are to be found in Brittany, as at Carnac, and in Scotland, and some now believe that Stonehenge is a solar and lunar observatory, built between 4,000 and 5,000 years ago.

Observatory instruments are not generally available, and so are beyond the scope of this book. Here astronomical models and time-telling devices will be considered.

Note on Hours
The development of modern communications has made the whole world accept the 24-hour clock, although many clocks and watches show a period of 12 hours only. The divisions of the day into double 12 or 24 parts are exceedingly old, although the day and night were not always divided as they are now. It is necessary to understand which system was used in order to interpret the lines and marks on the astrolabe, quadrant, and sundial.

Planetary Hours, so called because astrologers supposed each hour to be ruled by a planet, were also named 'unequal hours', 'temporal hours' or 'Jewish hours'. Here the periods of daylight and darkness are each divided into 12 hours, the key times being sunrise and sunset. This means that mid-day and mid-night are the sixth hour, and that the day and night hours are not of the same length. They can be equal only at the Vernal and Autumnal Equinoxes; at mid-summer in northern Europe, the night-hour could equal 40 minutes of our time, and the day-hour 80 minutes of our time. At mid-winter of course, these times would be reversed, with 80 for night and 40 for day.

Babylonian Hours, also 'Bohemian hours', belong to a system where the day plus night is divided into 24 equal hours, but they are numbered from sunrise to the next sunrise. Thus, the middle of the day would be at a different numbered hour as the year progressed.

Italian Hours are like Babylonian hours, but are numbered from sunset to the next sunset.

Uniform Hours. By the fourteenth century clocks with bells, and then with faces, began to be placed in churches and other important buildings, and since a mechanical clock must be regular in its movement a system of hours uniform in length came into general use. The rate of the clock, its accuracy, had to be checked by a sundial, and this necessitated new designs which would supersede the ancient mass-clocks scratched onto church walls by the Saxons and their successors.

Armillary Sphere

In Greek times, there were models of the Solar System, with the Earth at the centre, called armillary spheres: they were composed of hoops that linked the poles, the equator, and the ecliptic, and carried rings that showed the positions of the planets. It is thought that some of these were fitted with sights, but those still to be found in collections date from the sixteenth century onwards, and have no sights. An armillary sphere can be as much as 20 feet (6 m) in diameter, though one beautiful example made in 1720 by John Rowley of London, from silver and ebony, is only 6 inches (15 cm) in diameter. Armillary spheres were still produced in the eighteenth century to demonstrate the two world systems; the Greek, Ptolemaic, system, with the Earth at the centre, and the sixteenth-century Copernican system, which is Sun-centred, and which became the accepted model of our Solar System.

Astrolabe

In many ways this is the archetypal scientific instrument, because of its antiquity and remarkable sophistication. The astrolabe—the name means 'star-taking'—is a flat, circular instrument, usually of brass, occasionally of silver, which embodies a stereographic projection of the globe, and of the hemisphere of the heavens; a sort of flattened armillary sphere. The point of projection is nearly always the South Pole, and the plane of the projection the Equator. This is why scholars refer to the instrument as a planispheric astrolabe, in distinction to the spherical astrolabe, which is a model of the globe and the heavens, needing no lines of projection. Only one example of a spherical astrolabe is known to exist. The astrolabe was introduced to Europe through Spain by the Islamic peoples who occupied the north coast of Africa and part of Spain in the tenth century.

The astrolabe is thought to have had its origin in the Greek communities of philosophers and astronomers shortly before the beginning of the Christian era, and it continued to be made in Western Europe until the seventeenth century and until the twentieth century in some Islamic countries. This was because times of prayer had traditionally been determined by using an astrolabe. The earliest surviving astrolabes are Islamic, from Syrian workshops of the ninth century. In the tenth century, Persian astrolabes were being made in Isfahan which became an important centre for the craft. The Muslim conquest of Spain introduced the knowledge of astronomical and other scientific matters to that country. In the eleventh century the craft of the astrolabe maker was introduced, and when the Christians re-captured Toledo in 1085, the Europeans continued and developed the making of astrolabes and other instruments, and centres arose in France, Germany, the Netherlands, and England. The *Treatise on the Astrolabe* written in 1391 by Geoffrey Chaucer, the great English literary figure, is not only an excellent introduction to the use of the instrument, having been written for Chaucer's son Lewis, aged ten, but it is important as the first technical treatise written in the English native language.

Around the outer edge (called the limb) of an astrolabe is a scale divided into 360 degrees, and there is an alidade, or rule, with a pair of sighting vanes. A prominent star may be sighted and its altitude measured. A fretted disc (the rete), containing a number of star pointers, can then be turned until the measured star's pointer cuts or crosses the altitude circle on the stereographic projection. In this way, the pattern of the stars at a particular time is set on the model. If the day of the month is known it is possible to read off the time. The instrument is, in fact, an analogue computer. One must remember that the stars appear to rotate once in 24 hours. It is also possible to find the time of rising or setting of a given star, or of the Sun, at any date required. Another use is in surveying (Chapter 3), and a form of astrolabe was used by seamen (Chapter 2).

European astrolabes are now very rare and very expensive. Genuine

Islamic astrolabes are not infrequently sold by the main auction houses, and are not beyond hope of acquisition by a fairly modest collector. One should beware, however, of indiscriminate acquisition because of the large numbers that have been made this century, or even earlier, for the tourist trade. These are usually crude, although not always so, but they are invariably incorrect in the mathematics—the 'projection' is a collection of circles rather than truly stereographic. Since the inscriptions in Arabic are difficult to read except by an expert, it is always essential to take advice before purchase.

Sand-glass

Also called the hour-glass although it may tell half or quarter hours, the sand-glass is thought to have been invented in the Mediterranean area in the twelfth century. It may, indeed, be associated with the magnetic compass, which was used by seamen to plot magnetic bearings and distance on a portolan chart. Certainly, it has become popularly associated with navigation, 30 minutes being an interval timed on a course and noted on the traverse board (see Chapter 2). A half-minute sand-glass was also in use with a log-line for estimating a ship's speed. Other activities would have required a sand-glass, since the monastic disputation, the sermon, schools and law-courts all required the facility for simple timing. Quite small sand-glasses may be for timing eggs, or for a physician to time the pulse.

The sand-glass consists of two pear-shaped glass flasks, joined at the necks, and part filled with dry, uniform-grained sand. The frame that holds the glass has to be reversible, and is usually of wood, very simply, even crudely, made. Other frames may be in elaborately carved wood, ivory, or embossed and gilded metal. The flasks may be individually mounted for 60, 45, 30 or 15 minutes, or they may be united in a row of four.

The two separate flasks were joined at their necks with a perforated diaphragm between them, and then a seal was made with wax or putty, and bound with cord. This practice was changed in around 1725, when a perforated brass ball was put between the necks and the seal made by fusing the glass. By the end of the eighteenth century the double flask was blown as a single unit. The actual size is no indication of the time the sand will run, which is solely controlled by the size of the hole between the flasks and the grain size of the sand.

Unless the decoration is very elaborate, it is rarely possible to date or even give a country of origin to a sand-glass, because there is scarcely ever a maker's mark, and glass and plain wood are virtually undatable. This makes modern replicas, of which there are many, very easy to pass off as originals.

Quadrant

The quadrant is named from its shape, a quarter of a circle. The curved edge is divided from 0° to 90°, and at the right-angle, the apex, a cord is attached with a small weight of lead or brass at the other end. On one straight edge is mounted a pair of metal pin-hole sights. By holding the quadrant vertically, and aligning the sights on the Sun or a star, the angle of elevation can be read off the degree scale by the position of the cord, which is kept in a vertical line by the weight. This very simple instrument, in its variations, is used for navigation, surveying, and for time-telling. Quadrants can be classified as follows.

Altitude. The plain quadrant, with 0°–90° arc, with plumb-line, for taking altitudes with degree scale and plumb-line.

Gunner's. Used by artillery officers for setting the angle of a gun barrel.

Gunter's. Invented by Edmund Gunter in 1623, chiefly for time-telling.

Horary. Solely for time-telling.

Islamic. One side has an astrolabe quadrant and the other a sinecal quadrant with arcs of sines, cosines, etc.

The horary quadrant is mediaeval in origin. The now exceedingly rare *quadrans vetus* (old quadrant) was of brass, with a sliding, curved plate (cursor) that moved in a slot above the degree arc. This cursor had engraved on it a Zodiac scale and a solar declination scale. Above this the rest of the quadrant had a diagram of planetary hour (unequal hour) lines. The cursor was set to the latitude of the observer, the plumb-line was held over the date on the declination scale, and a small bead on the plumb-line was moved till it cut the 6 o'clock line (mid-day). With the plumb-line free, the sights were pointed at the Sun so that the shadow of the foresight fell right over the backsight, when the position of the bead told the time in unequal hours. This is the mode of action of all horary quadrants. Later they ceased to be universal and had fixed scales for a particular latitude, and hour lines for Italian or Babylonian hours. A shadow square for trigonometrical surveying was frequently added.

Gunter's quadrant, or Gunter's astrolabe quadrant, was first described by Edmund Gunter, Professor of Astronomy at Gresham College in London, in his book *De Sectore et Radio*, published in 1623. A stereographic projection of the Equator (or the equinoctial line as it is also named), the tropics, the ecliptic, and the horizon, in the manner of an astrolabe projection, is engraved on brass or on a copper printing plate for paper versions. The arc is divided into $90°$ as before, and on the left hand edge is a solar declination scale, $0°-23\frac{1}{2}°$, which is the angular distance the Sun moves from the Equinox (when the Sun crosses the Equator) to the Solstice (mid-summer or mid-winter); it is, in fact, the angle at which the axis of the Earth is tilted in relation to the orbit round the Sun. The Sun's meridian (noon) altitude on a given date depends also on the latitude, and so the meridian altitude at mid-summer at a latitude of $52°$ North, is the co-latitude $(90° - 52° = 38°)$ plus the declination, $23\frac{1}{2}°$, giving $61\frac{1}{2}°$. At mid-winter, the meridian altitude of the Sun is $14\frac{1}{2}°$ $(38° - 23\frac{1}{2}°)$. The arc running through zero on the declination scale represents the Equator or equinoctial, and the arc at $23\frac{1}{2}°$ represents either of the tropics. The dotted line that starts from the zero and reaches the bottom right hand corner of the instrument is the ecliptic, that is the Earth's orbit or the course through which the Sun appears to travel during the year. The signs of the Zodiac are marked on it. The other dotted line that goes from the zero to nearly half way along the bottom arc represents the horizon.

On the left of centre are two sets of hour lines (here in modern, equal hours) that converge on the equinoctial line; those curving to the left are for the winter half of the year, and those curving right are for the summer half. On the right of centre are lines of the Sun's azimuth, where $0°$ is the meridian, and $90°$ is the East-West line. By measuring the Sun's altitude, and setting the time bead, the azimuth (horizon angle) of the Sun can be found by the position of the bead among the curves when the plumb-line is positioned over the complementary angle to the altitude on the degree scale. Again there are two sets of curves; those going left are for summer, and those going right are for winter use.

To tell the time by the Sun, the bead is positioned on the line according to the declination. This can be taken from the scale to the left, or more accurately from the position of the Sun in the ecliptic. The altitude of the Sun is then measured using the sights. For example, on 20 April the Sun enters the sign of Taurus, giving a declination of $11°$ $14'$ (in the seventeenth century the date would have been 10 April by the Julian calendar), and if the altitude is $36°$, the plumb-line is placed over this angle when the bead will cut the hour line marked 9 and 3. To decide

17

whether it is morning or afternoon, the Sun will be rising or lowering as time goes on. Time at night can be found by taking the altitude of one of the stars whose right ascension is marked on the instrument and making a simple calculation. The month scale used with the degree scale gives the Sun's meridian altitude on any day, so, conversely, the date can be found by measuring the meridian altitude. Various other calculations can also be made with this ingenious instrument.

To find the latitude for which the quadrant was designed, supposing that it is not marked, a line is taken from the apex through the 12 o'clock point and extended to the degree scale, where the co-latitude is found. That is, for a measured angle of 38°, the latitude is 52° (90° − 38°).

There were other mathematicians and surveyors who devised quadrants, but the Gunter's quadrant is frequently met with by collectors. Most date from 1650 to 1750. Being pocket sized, they were popular as a convenient time teller and almanac. In addition, they were used for teaching purposes in universities. Sizes are from about 4 inches (10 cm) to 6 and 9 inches (15 and 23 cm), and examples can be found in boxwood, ivory, and often in brass. There are printed versions stuck onto oak boards. The back of a Gunter's quadrant may either be blank, have a map of the prominent constellations, have a type of nocturnal on a rotating disc, or have a sundial with a slot for a style to fit in.

Nocturnal

The nocturnal (*nocturlabe* in French) is a simple instrument for giving a rough indication of the time, perhaps to a quarter of an hour, during the night. Its use depends on being able to see the Pole Star and the Great Bear (Ursa major) or Plough, and on the fact that the stars appear to rotate about the Pole once in 24 hours (less 4 minutes each day). In appearance, it looks like a small, circular, table-tennis bat with a calendar scale engraved on it. Rotating over this is a disc marked with two periods of twelve hours (sometimes with night hours only, 8 pm to 8 am). The hour positions are usually notched for counting by feel, the 12 o'clock having a larger notch. Above this disc is a long rotating pointer, and the central rivet has a hole. To tell the time, the 12 o'clock is set to the date, the instrument is held upright, the Pole Star sighted through the rivet, and the pointer turned to be in line with the Guards of the Bear, that is, the two prominent stars α and β in the constellation that align with the Pole Star. The time is then shown by the pointer cutting the hour disc.

The nocturnal was described in sixteenth century texts, and examples dating from about 1500 exist. Italian and French models purporting to be late sixteenth and early seventeenth century are quite likely to be nineteenth century replicas. Dutch and English models of the late seventeenth and eighteenth centuries, in brass or boxwood, are generally authentic. Few are signed. Sometimes there is provision for using the star β in the Lesser Bear (Ursa minor) as well, and marks such as 'GB' and 'LB', or 'Both Bears' can be found stamped into the wood.

Sundials

Of all the mathematical instruments that may be collected, the sundial is the one most commonly met with. The chief reason for this is that the mechanical clock absolutely required a sundial to check that it was keeping correct time. It is probably true to say that the great numbers of sundials made in the seventeenth and eighteenth centuries matched the equally large numbers of clocks in general use. Every church required a sundial to ensure that the turret clock kept time. Similarly, in the late seventeenth century and throughout the eighteenth, most country houses had a horizontal dial, usually mounted on a pedestal in the garden. Anyone who possessed a watch would very likely also own a pocket sundial, and on occasion, the two were combined in the same case. Every locality has its own time, and consequently the local time at Oxford, for example, is five minutes slower than Greenwich, because Oxford is $1\frac{1}{4}°$ West of Greenwich in longitude. At Bristol, the local time is 10 minutes behind Greenwich.

Two developments occured in the 1830s that quite independently transformed the situation. The new railways needed to keep the same time along all routes, and this could conveniently be done by means of the electric telegraph, which was first used in 1837. By the mid-nineteenth century, the National Telegraph Company had offices in most towns, and exhibited a clock that told Greenwich time. From then on, the sundial ceased to be of any practical importance, and remained merely as a decorative object.

Most sundials function by casting a shadow onto a marked out surface; the edge of a piece of metal, a rod, or a string may be used to cast the shadow. Some work by letting the Sun's rays pass through a small hole, so that the time is read by a spot of light. The object that casts the shadow is called the gnomon (from the Greek word meaning 'indicator'), or the style. In general, the gnomon is arranged to be parallel to the axis of the Earth. The plate that receives the shadow can be parallel to the horizon, or vertical to this plane, or in practically any position, provided that it is engraved specifically for that orientation. But some dials have the shadow received on a ring, which is parallel to the Earth's Equator. The equinoctial ring dial is an example of this, where the hours are easy to mark out, because they are at $15°$ intervals round the ring. Looking at a large collection of sundials in a museum, one cannot but be amazed by the variety of protrusions and apertures that have been devised for use in time-telling. One amusing example allows the heel of a Dutch wooden clog to cast a shadow along the sole. Although the principle of a sundial is so simple, there are many types still to be found today, each having its own peculiar characteristic and descriptive name. The most common of these types are described below.

Horizontal This is the common, garden sundial, which can also be found in small versions (see Butterfield dial below). The hour lines are engraved on a round or square plate of brass, bronze or slate, and in the middle is the gnomon of thin metal, whose straight edge is parallel with the axis of the Earth when the dial is set in its position. The hour lines have to be calculated for a particular latitude, and this is usually engraved on the South side. The latitude angle can easily be found by measuring the angle between the gnomon and the plate. A postcard or similar can be placed behind the gnomon, and a pencil run along it; a protractor can then be set over the angle. When clocks became more accurate from the early eighteenth century, the seasonal variations in the Sun's times became important because the clock keeps mean time whereas the sundial does not. This is because the Earth has an elliptical orbit, not a circular one. To allow for this, the equation of time is indicated against the date on a ring round the dial plate. Periods are marked: Watch Slow and Watch Fast; the variation can be as great as 18 minutes.

Good quality garden dials were made by established mathematical instrument makers, such as Elias Allen, John Marke, Edmund Culpeper, Benjamin Scott, Benjamin Martin, Peter Dollond. There are many modern horizontal garden dials, some of which are purely ornamental. Good quality replicas were made, particularly in the 1920s, that seem at first glance to be older. Beware of any dial with a Sun's face, and a tag such as 'I tell ye sunny hours', or 'Set me right and treat me well, And I the time to you will tell'.

Vertical This is the kind very frequently found on the wall of a church, probably incised into the stone of the structure. Other examples may be of painted wood, brass, sandstone or slate. Those that were made to face due South may look like horizontal dials if removed from the wall.

But a vertical dial cannot receive the Sun's light before 6 am or after 6 pm at any time of year, so the missing hour lines reveal its type. Small versions are found on diptych dials (see page 22). If the wall is not due South, the gnomon is skewed, and the 12 o'clock line is at an angle to the edge of the plate.

Polyhedral This type can combine horizontal with vertical in several orientations, and can include plates at an angle with the vertical. Twelve-sided solids can have each face fitted up with a gnomon, and such can be found as monumental dials in grand settings. Small brass and even pottery versions are known, a popular late eighteenth-century type being a cube. This was produced in Germany by D. Beringer, among others, and had coloured printed paper dial faces stuck on to the wooden cube.

Compass A horizontal dial over a magnetic compass, this type goes back to the fifteenth century. The dial plate has been cut away to reveal the compass card and needle, and the gnomon is hinged for packing. A popular dial, the compass dial was usually quite small, and is still made today as a novelty. Andreas Vogler of Augsburg made them in the eighteenth century.

Magnetic Compass In name, this is easy to confuse with the compass dial (see above), but in the case of the magnetic compass, the dial plate with its gnomon is the actual compass card. Below the pivoted card, and fixed to it, is the magnetic needle. This means that the dial is self-orientating; at least, it will orientate to the magnetic North, and a correction of some sort will be necessary for declinations. These small dials became quite popular in the first half of the nineteenth century, being produced by Fraser, and S. Porter, both in London, and they are still made today for adventurous small boys.

Butterfield A form of horizontal dial with an adjustable angle to the gnomon and a compass, this semi-universal type is named after Michael Butterfield (1635–1724), who worked in Paris at the end of the seventeenth century. A very popular pocket dial, it was made frequently in silver, but also in brass; the characteristic shape has an eight-sided plate, with one pair of sides longer than the others; an oval version is also found. French-made models have four hour rings, one inside the other, for latitudes 43°, 46°, 49° and 52°. The gnomon can be raised to suit these latitudes, the degree pointer being the beak of a bird. English-made Butterfield-type dials have only one hour scale for 52°, but the bird pointer is copied. A small compass is incorporated in the plate at the South end. The plate is supported by the base of the compass box and two feet. On the underside are lists of towns and their latitudes. A great many were made during the eighteenth century, and signed by many different craftsmen in Paris and London. Butterfield's name was forged in the eighteenth century, and it seems that this may also occur today. Names found on these dials include: Butterfield à Paris; P. Le Maire à Paris; Le Maire Fils; Macquart; Cadot; E. Culpeper, London; J. Simons, London; Richard Whitehead, London (c. 1690); Nicholas Bion, Paris; Charles Bloud, Dieppe.

Inclining This is a portable universal dial, based on the compass dial. Some are small enough for the pocket, others are suitable to be placed on a window ledge. A large compass is in the base, for quick orientation. The hour plate is hinged, and can be set at an angle read from a curved arm fitted to one side of the base. This dial is handy for travellers, and the underside of the base usually has a list of principal towns with their latitudes. The gnomon and the arm are hinged for packing flat. The principle is that any horizontal dial can be used at another latitude provided the shadow-casting edge of the gnomon is parallel to the Earth's axis. English examples from the early eighteenth century were made by Bryan Scott, Jonathan Sisson, Heath & Wing, and Dollond. Others include: Johann Martin (c. 1700), Augsburg; Pierre Le Maire (c. 1750), Paris; Francis Morgan (c. 1780), St. Petersburg.

Analemmatic This is the name given to a special form of horizontal dial, which is so made that it is self-orientating. In this connection, the word analemma signifies the table of the Sun's daily declination from tropic to tropic ($23\frac{1}{2}°$N to $23\frac{1}{2}°$S) and back during the year. In addition to a horizontal dial for a given latitude, there is another dial with a vertical gnomon that is attached to a slider which can set the gnomon to any date in the year—this is, in fact, the analemma. Around this is an hour scale in the shape of an ellipse, and when the sundial is positioned so that both hour scales tell the *same* time, then it is orientated to the meridian, and the time is known. Pierre Sevin of Paris made such a dial in about 1670, and Thomas Tuttell of Charing Cross, London, introduced it to Britain, and he described it in a little book published in 1698. It is a fairly rare type; however, a fine example exists by John Bird, the famous eighteenth-century astronomical instrument maker, and Victorian examples are known.

Diptych The word means anything folded so as to have two leaves and here two plates are hinged together, and in use are opened out to make a right angle: a string gnomon is thus drawn taut and the shadow falls on to a horizontal dial as well as a vertical dial. These are cut on the

22

inner faces of the plates. There is usually a magnetic compass, and pin gnomon dials for Italian and Babylonian hours. On the outside of the top plate may be a wind rose and pointer, and on the underside of the bottom plate is customarily a lunar disc with calendrical information. The peak output for this type was at Nuremberg in the late sixteenth and early seventeenth centuries, and ivory was the traditional material for their construction. They vary in size and can be elaborately decorated, the cuts being filled in with a black, blue, red or green colouring agent. Attractive and ancient, they command high prices today, although they are not particularly rare. Famous makers include Georg Hartmann, Hans Tucher, Hans Troschel, Jacob Karner, who used as a mark the figure 3, and Lienhart Miller. Late eighteenth and early nineteenth-century German versions in wood with printed scales were also produced in large numbers, some showing the latitudes of principal towns in the United States of America.

Magnetic Azimuth, or Bloud This is a form of diptych dial, nearly always in ivory, which was produced by Charles Bloud and others working in Dieppe, chiefly during the period 1650–70. There may be a string gnomon dial, but generally the top plate is a polar dial. This means that the plate is propped up according to the latitude so that it is parallel to the Equator, and a rod is inserted at the centre of the hour circle. The main feature is the magnetic azimuth dial, so called because when the dial is turned so that the shadow of the top plate falls exactly over the lower, the magnetic needle points to the time on an elliptical, pewter, hour scale. To allow for the declination of the Sun, this hour scale has to move in a slot, and this is effected by turning a metal disc on the underside of the bottom plate to the appropriate date. This disc is always engraved with a perpetual calendar. This type of dial works effectively only when the magnetic declination is zero, which was the case for Dieppe, London, and nearby areas in 1657. Names of other Dieppe craftsmen include Jacques Senecal and Ephraim Senecal.

Equatorial or Equinoctial (also referred to as Augsburg dial) The hour scale is made to be parallel to the Equator, and when the Sun is exactly over the Equator it is the time of the Vernal or the Autumnal Equinox, hence the names given to this dial. Being universal (i.e. adjustable for latitude) it was a very popular type made in large numbers, especially in Germany, during the late seventeenth and eighteenth centuries. It is generally made of brass, and in its German form is often eight-sided. In the base is a magnetic compass, and on the South side there is nearly always a levelling bob in a hinged frame. On the West side is a curved arm engraved with degrees of latitude. The hour scale is cut on the inside of a thin ring, and since it is equatorial, the divisions are all equal, at 15° to one hour. The gnomon is a needle on a cross bar which can be turned so that the needle is at right angles to the ring. Everything hinges for packing into a fishskin case to go in the pocket. A perpetual calendar can be an addition to the lid of the case. Some of the eighteenth-century Augsburg craftsmen who made this type of dial are Nicolaus Rugendas, Johann Georg Vogler, Andreas Vogler, Ludwig Theodatus Müller. Parisian makers of the eighteenth century are Claude Langlois, and Macquart & Cadot.

Crescent This is a variation on the equinoctial dial, where the hour circle is divided in two and the two parts are transposed so they virtually touch at the 6 o'clock points, making a double crescent. The gnomon is also in the form of a crescent, with the tips casting the shadow. This crescent is held at the middle by a screw, which can move in a slot with a declination scale. This adjustment for the time of year means that the shadow of the tip of the gnomon falls exactly on the hour ring, so the instrument is turned until this occurs, making the dial self-orientating, which obviates the need for a compass. There is a levelling bob or spirit level and adjustment screws in the base plate. A most decorative dial, it can be made in brass, gilded brass or silver, and seems to have had its origin in Augsburg in the late seventeenth century. Notable makers are Johann Martin, Johann Willebrand, Christoff Schener. The signature 'Masig a London' means a Martin dial sold by his agent. French models are known, but the crescent was never popular in Britain.

Universal Equinoctial Ring Dial This is one of the most elegant of all sundials; it is self-orientating and universal, and accurate. Since the hour ring is in the plane of the Equator, the accuracy of the scale is high because the divisions are equal, and with large models, say one foot (30 cm) in diameter, made by the best craftsmen, time can be read to about one minute. There are three principal parts: outer, meridian ring; inner, hour ring; central bar. The meridian ring has a suspension ring adjustable for latitude. The hour ring is pivoted at the 12 o'clock positions to the outer and is set at right angles to it. It is divided into 24 hours on the inner side. The bar is pivoted to brackets fixed to the outer ring. This bar has a slot with a declination scale, months on one side and the signs of the Zodiac on the other. In the slot is an index with a pin-hole. A spot of light from this hole is allowed to fall on the hour scale by turning the instrument. When the spot is exactly on the scale, the time is given and the outer ring is in the plane of the meridian—North-South.

The back may have a solar altitude scale 0°–90°, used with a pin pushed in a hole in the outer ring. This type was invented around 1600, possibly by the English mathematician William Oughtred. Just about every mathematical instrument maker has his name on examples of this type of dial, and it was made all over Europe.

Larger versions are known, mounted on an azimuth plate with a pair of spirit levels and three adjusting screws, and a magnetic compass. Thomas Heath in the mid-eighteenth century favoured this model.

Ring or Poke This is the simplest of dials, but the accuracy is poor. Made as a wide ring of brass, like a wrist bangle, it has a sliding collar with a pin-hole to let a spot of sunlight fall on the graduated inner side of the ring when suspended vertically. The collar adjusts to the solar declination. Simpler versions have a fixed hole and two scales for winter and summer; others have a hole on each side of the suspension and two seasonal scales opposite them. A cheap dial, it was popular during the seventeenth and eighteenth centuries among country people who kept it in their poke, or pocket. Not infrequently they are literally unearthed. French, Italian, German, and English versions exist, frequently unsigned. L. Proctor of Sheffield seems to have had a good trade in these dials in around 1800. Other English ones are signed by initials only: E.E.; I.H.; T.W.

Pillar, Cylinder, or Shepherd's The hour scale is marked on the outside of a cylinder which stands vertically. The gnomon projects horizontally from the top, and when not in use is kept inside the pillar. The depth of the scale varies from winter to summer, and the gnomon has to be set over a month or Zodiac scale. A pillar dial can be very simple indeed, plain boxwood with carved lines, a type in use in the Pyrenees until the twentieth century. Others may be of wood with printed scales, and a few are in ivory, made in Dieppe during the eighteenth century.

Scafe, Cup-dial This is one of the oldest known forms of sundial, Roman examples having been preserved. Here the hour lines are engraved on the inner surface of a hemisphere or even a metal goblet. The gnomon is vertical in general, but it may be parallel to the polar axis. The tip tells the time. Shallow scafes are to be found on some ivory diptych dials. Italian examples from the sixteenth century are known, in particular by Alexander Ravillius in ivory, dated 1537, and Hieronimus Vulparia, 1588. Georg Hartmann of Nuremburg made one in brass dated 1539.

Cannon This is a horizontal dial, usually on marble or stone, with a miniature cannon and two brackets supporting a burning lens. The

25

bracket arms are set to the solar declination, so that when it is noon the burning beam of light fires the gun. Some large specimens are for use in ports or camps—the noon-day gun—but most examples are only 3-9 inches (7-21 cm). The cannon dial was patented by Victor Chevalier (1770-1841), an instrument maker of Paris. In 1880 they were offered for sale at 3 guineas (£3.15) by Negretti & Zambra of London. A large model is signed by F. Amuel of Berlin, and another German product is no bigger than a pocket watch.

Dipleidoscope In March 1842, Edward John Dent, the noted chronometer maker, patented a device for noting the meridian passage of the

Checking noon on a pocket watch by means of a dipleidoscope, 1843.

Sun with great accuracy. The invention consisted of a hollow right-angled prism with two sides silvered and one of glass. The meridian transit was known by the coincidence of two images of the Sun by single and double reflection, one from the top glass and the other from both mirrors. Of course, the base of the instrument had to be accurately levelled and orientated, but with this done, the time could be had to seconds. The instrument was made in portable and fixed versions. Dent cannot have profited from his novelty because the new electric telegraph soon replaced the need for an accurate time check in the form of a sundial.

Planetarium

Any instrument that shows the various motions of the bodies in the solar system is called a planetarium. It is a descendant of the armillary sphere. Small ivory balls represent the planets, and they are supported on brass wires, with long rods to a collar round a central pivot. The rods have to be pushed round by hand with the wooden models, and by a crank and gearing with the brass 'drum' type, devised by Benjamin Martin in 1747. Some are very large indeed, 4 feet (1.2 m) or so in diameter with elaborate clockwork mechanisms, craftsman-made cases and glazed covers. The last kind is usually called in Britain a *Grand Orrery*. The other planetaria are often termed *orreries*. They are named after Charles Boyle, 4th Earl of Orrery, who had a planetary model made for him by John Rowley in 1712. Rowley had been influenced by a clockwork device constructed by Thomas Tompion and George Graham in about 1709, which had a small globe of the Earth and an ivory Moon, to show both the daily and annual motions round the Sun; strictly, this is a tellurium, but the naming of these astronomical models is confused, and orrery has become the generic term. Planetaria were also sold with alternative systems to be placed on the central axis; a large brass ball for the Sun was always superimposed. The planetary system was removed, to be replaced by a 'tellurium', the Sun-Earth system, or by a 'lunarium', the Sun-Earth-Moon system stressing the Moon's orbit. There are sometimes hybrid instruments with combinations of all three variations permanently arranged.

George Adams of London exported to Holland in 1790 a 'drum' type planetarium which showed Mercury, Venus, Earth and Moon, Mars and Jupiter with 4 moons, Saturn with ring and 8 moons, Uranus with 2 moons. The number of planets and of moons helps dating around the end of the eighteenth century. Herschel discovered Uranus in 1781,

27

and its two moons in 1787. Saturn was found to have a seventh moon in 1789, but its eighth moon was not discovered till 1848 (Adams had anticipated that Herschel would discover the eighth, and made his instrument accordingly). Neptune was discovered in 1846. A knowledge of elementary astronomy was in great demand during the early nineteenth century, and a large number of planetaria exist from this time. The usual form is a round wooden disc, covered with a printed and coloured sheet, showing the calendar and Zodiac, and giving information about distances from the Sun and the occurrence of comets. Sizes vary, some being no more than toys. Names associated with this type include W & S Jones, William Cary, William Harris, Newton & Sons.

Globes

The history of charts, maps and globes is a specialist study which though connected with navigation and surveying cannot be dealt with fully here. Large globes of two-foot diameter or more were used by navigators to help solve problems in sailing. Pairs of globes, one of the Earth and one of the constellations—terrestrial and celestial—were regular furnishings in a library from the seventeenth century on. During the eighteenth and nineteenth centuries they had a place in nearly every school, and common sizes were 1, $1\frac{1}{2}$ and 2 foot (30, 45 and 60 cm).

Small pocket globes, from 2–3 inches (5–8 cm) in diameter, are available to collectors. They are made from pasteboard or wood, covered with gores printed from engraved copper plates, hand-coloured. At the poles are brass pins that support the globe in its case. This is composed of two hemispheres hinged together, which are covered on the outside with black fishskin, and on the inside with the celestial sphere, showing the constellations.

The pocket globe was first produced by the London mathematician and hydrographer, Joseph Moxon, who also sold instruments, maps and globes. He produced, among others, nine-inch and pocket globes before 1700. In the eighteenth century the trade in these small globes was continued by Charles Price, John Senex, Robert Cushee, James Ferguson, Nathaniel Hill, George Adams and N. Lane. During the early nineteenth century, important makers and retailers are Dudley Adams, William Cary, John Newton, Charles Schmalcalder and James Cox. The actual manufacturers of these globes will have been fewer than the names found on them, and this is particularly true for retailers in provincial towns.

The pocket globe had as its chief use the instruction in geography and astronomy of school children; but there was probably a subsidiary use as an *aide mémoire* to any reasonably educated person who perhaps could not afford a large globe. Pocket globes had their period of highest production at the time of the remarkable voyages of discovery, for example, by Captain Cook to Australia and New Zealand, and George Vancouver to the West coast of America. The little globes may have acted as conversation pieces as each new edition charted a new track of Cook's, or a newly defined coastline. It is in this way that the globes can be dated, even if the engraving of the date of the original production has not been altered. George Anson sailed round the world in 1744, Cook's three voyages occurred between 1768 and 1774, and Vancouver explored Western Canada in 1790–95. The other factor in dating is the development of the coasts of Australia and North America. The island of Tasmania was shown connected to the mainland until 1792. On a Hill globe of 1754, the coast of Alaska is missing, and Greenland is joined to Eastern North America.

2
Navigational Instruments

While a ship is sailing along the coast, the determination of its position is no great problem. Beginning at its port of departure, which has a known longitude and latitude, the course and the distance can be plotted on the sea-chart. The course is steered, and the coastline and marker points, headlands, churches, rocks, are noted. After a time, the new position can be checked by bearings on the shore. With a ship, its way through the water is different from the distance travelled over the sea bottom because of currents and tidal flow, and drift caused by the wind.

In the open sea, out of sight of land, a different sort of navigation has to be applied. The latitude (the angular distance from the Equator $0°$ to the Pole $90°$) can be measured by a quadrant or cross-staff by taking the elevation above the horizon of the Pole Star. The altitude of the Sun at noon, when it crosses the meridian, can be taken by a quadrant or sea astrolabe, fore-staff or octant. Knowing the day of the month, the altitude, and hence the latitude, can be found from tables. The longitude is difficult: this is the angle around the globe, and nowadays the prime meridian is taken as the longitude of Greenwich, $0°$; New York is $74°$ West, and Hamburg is $10°$ East. Longitude can be measured by a clock, because if you know the time at your port of departure, and can find out the local time, say noon, by the Sun, then the difference in time gives you the longitude, because one hour equals $15°$ of longitude. But clockwork mechanisms were not good enough to withstand the ship's motion, and changes in temperature, until after the mid-eighteenth century, when John Harrison perfected the marine chronometer. Before this, seamen had to rely on the compass, the log-line, and the traverse board to keep a tally. Of course, charts and globes, with scales and dividers, were used by navigators to help solve the problems, which needed more skills and hence training as the centuries rolled by.

When the Portuguese, during the early fifteenth century, began to explore the coast of West Africa, it was initially by coastal navigation. But when India was to be reached, instrumental navigation became necessary. The Portuguese Prince, Henry the Navigator, founded a training workshop at Sagres for officers. Here were brought mathematicians and astronomers and cartographers to found the nautical science of navigation, to devise instruments, and to draw up charts.

In the middle of the fifteenth century, Portuguese sailors would use the plain, altitude quadrant for angle measurements. The astronomical quadrant is known from classical times; for ship use they were about ten inches (25 cm) in radius, were engraved with a scale from $0°$ to $90°$, had a pair of pin-hole sights, and a plumb-bob, which marked the angle indicated by the sights. The Portuguese navigators knew that they could return to Lisbon by taking the winds out into the Atlantic until the latitude of Lisbon ($38° 42'$) was reached, as shown by the altitude of the Pole Star. Then it remained to run East 'down the latitude'. In spite of the later instruments, the quadrant found favour among some sailors until the seventeenth century, and was still used on shore till the eighteenth century. Of course, near the Equator the Pole Star is too close to the northern horizon to be of use, so the altitude of the Sun became the important measure.

Sea Astrolabe

For plotting the altitude of the Sun near the meridian this instrument came into use around 1470. It is a development of the much earlier astronomer's planispheric astrolabe (see Chapter 1). The sea astrolabe has the same angular divisions on the outer ring, but is not always divided right round, and it has an alidade, or sighting rule, but here the similarity ends. The sea astrolabe is very heavy, especially at the bottom, and is made of brass or bronze. The weight helps to keep it steady, and there are considerable portions cut away to reduce wind resistance, which would otherwise make its use harder. The instrument is held by its ring, just above the $90°$ mark, (sometimes $0°$), and the alidade is turned until a beam of sunlight from the hole in the upper vane exactly falls into the hole in the lower. The angle of elevation of the Sun can now be read from the scale on the rim. The instrument illustrated (Plate 12), now in the Dundee Museum, is the oldest surviving dated example, and is marked 1555. It has a diameter of nearly nine inches (22cm), and it weighs 6 lb 6 oz (2.86 kg). Although the sea astrolabe is very rare, only 35 were known in 1979, it may sometimes be found in wrecks (e.g. off Northern Ireland in 1968) or among rocks (e.g. Lyme Bay, Dorset, in 1967). These will have been equipment on ships of the Spanish Armada.

31

De partibus menfurae feu Speciebus Geometriae practicae. Caput vndecimum.

Enfura eft longitudo finita: quae ignotam loco
rum diftantiam fenfibili experimento menfurat. Cuius ptes
feu famofæ quantitates/quibus Geometer vtitur funt Gra
num bordei/Digit⁹/Vncia/ Palmus/Dichas/Spithames
pes/Sefquipes/Gradus/ paffus fimpler/paffus dupler quê Geome
tricum appellare libuit/Cubitus feu vlna/ pertica quem plures radium
vocant/Stadiû/Leuca/Miliare italicum/Miliare germanicum. ꝛc.

The method of using a cross-staff for determining longitude by lunar dis-
tances, from Petrus Apianus, Cosmographia seu descriptio totius orbis,
1524.

Cross-staff

As an astronomical and then as a surveying instrument, the cross-staff may be traced from the description published in 1328 by the southern French mathematician and astronomer the Rabbi Levi ben Gerson. His instrument, which depends on the principle of similar triangles, was called Jacob's staff after the Biblical story in Genesis 32:10. It consists of a rectangular staff, five or six feet (1.5 or 1.8 m) in length, with a perpendicular vane that moves over it. The staff is graduated trigonometrically so that angles can be measured by holding the staff to the eye and moving the vane until its ends are level with the points that are to be measured. The instrument was introduced into England by John Dee in the 1550s, when it was developed to measure the angles between stars and to measure the heights of buildings or the angles between topographical features. Early in the sixteenth century it was in use as a seaman's navigational instrument, its use being pioneered by the Portuguese. Originally with one vane or cross, seamen added other vanes because for their use the staff had to be shorter, about $2\frac{1}{2}$ foot (75 cm) long; so long, medium, and short vanes were used, of about 15, 10 and 6 inches (37, 25 and 15 cm). The staff was calibrated directly in degrees for ease of use on board ship. The typical measurement was to find the latitude by measuring the altitude of the Pole Star above the horizon. The Sun's altitude could also be found, but this required the observer to face the Sun, with the result that its light was in his eyes. To avoid this, the back-staff was devised, and the cross-staff became known as the fore-staff.

Back-staff

This was invented by the English captain, John Davis, in about 1594, and was intended to be an improvement on the quadrant, sea astrolabe and cross-staff for finding the meridian altitude of the Sun. The back-staff was also known as the Davis quadrant, and as the English quadrant by continental seamen. The name quadrant arises because 90 degrees can be measured although there is no 90° arc. The instrument looks like a large triangle with a 30° arc at one end, and a small, 60° arc at the other. One-sided vanes with pin-holes move over these arcs, and at the end opposite the large arc is a push-on vane with a slit through which the horizon could be viewed. By adjusting the vanes the Sun's angle can be found.

The cross-staff is very rare, but the back-staff is not; eighteenth-century examples are met with in sales, and are usually signed and dated. Both types of staff have been replicated and it is not always easy to distinguish them.

Octant

The back-staff was transformed into the octant by John Hadley who published his invention in the pages of the *Philosophical Transactions of the Royal Society* in 1731. The novelty was the use of a mirror mounted over the pivot of a radial arm that moved over a graduated arc. Viewing was through a pin-hole sight at a half-silvered mirror, which caught the reflection of the Sun from the first mirror on one half, while the horizon could be seen through the clear half, so 'bringing the Sun down' to the horizon.

The name of this instrument sometimes causes confusion because it can measure 90°, a quadrant of a circle; the actual arc, however, occupies only one eighth of a circle, an octant. The reason is that the use of a mirror halves the angle through which the radial arm moves, although the arc itself is calibrated from 0° to 90°.

The octant came into general use after 1750, and it continued until about 1900, and later in coastal navigation. The Deutsche Seewarte was certifying wooden octants until 1925. It varies little in form, but the examples vary in size from $7\frac{1}{2}$ to 20 inches (19 to 50 cm). The frame is mahogany in the earlier examples, and ebony after 1800. The scale can be engraved on boxwood, ivory, or brass. The early ones have transversals, or diagonal scales, to measure fractions of a degree; verniers came later. Those verniers with a central zero are usually before 1780, and those with a zero on the right are after this date. Often an octant is engraved with both the name of the maker and of the owner; occasionally there is a date as well.

Sextant

When the new method for finding the longitude at sea by measuring the distances of certain stars from the Moon—lunar distance method—was brought in after 1767, the greater accuracy required led to the development of the sextant for use at sea after about 1770. The name refers to the actual arc, which occupies a sixth of a circle, and not to the angle that can be measured. As with the octant, the mirror halves the angle, and the actual arc is calibrated from 0° to 120°. Much more accurate than the octant, and therefore more expensive, sextants were used by officers of the more wealthy companies such as the East India Company. Some early examples are in ebony; mostly the construction is in brass. The greatest practitioners in precision instrument-making divided the sextant: John Bird (died 1776), Jesse Ramsden (died 1800), Edward Troughton (died 1836).

From 1800 onwards, sextants were made in large numbers; English products were sold through agents in Denmark, in the United States, and elsewhere, and there were manufacturers in Paris, Hamburg, Amsterdam and many other places. Great efforts were made to produce sextants that could be highly accurate wherever they were used in the world, and whatever the conditions. The original brass bar construction gave way to various strutted constructions which include grids, ovals with straight bars, and three circles between the two outer limbs and the arc. Another type was the double plated form, where two thin plates are held together by a series of cylinders (pillar sextant), patented in 1788 by Troughton. On occasion, Troughton would give his sextants scales divided on silver, gold, or even platinum. A well-known Dutch contemporary of Troughton was Gerard Hulst van Keulen of Amsterdam, who produced fine sextants, which he numbered serially, as did Ramsden, Berge, Troughton, and Troughton & Simms.

Reflecting Circle

The ultimate in accuracy, exceeding that of the sextant, was given by the reflecting circle. This was invented by the German astronomer, Tobias Mayer, in the 1750s so that his method of finding the longitude by lunar distances could be as accurate as possible. The principle is the same as that used in the sextant, but the arc is taken into a full circle of 360°. The sighting telescope and the horizon mirror can be moved on an arm to any position on the circle where it is clamped, and the index arm turned to effect the apparent conjunction of the two objects being measured. The angle is the difference between the readings, and for extra accuracy verniers are fitted to the arms. The measurements can be repeated at different parts of the circle, which again helps to reduce errors of collimation and scale division. With the circles made by Edward Troughton from 1796, three index arms with verniers were fitted, and an average taken of the three readings.

The reflecting circle was more popular with the navies of France and Germany than with British seamen, and the extra cost limited the market. The instrument is also known as the Borda circle after the French inventor, Chevalier de Borda, who published a description of it in 1787. Other types were also made during the nineteenth century, and some of the principal makers were: Berge, Dollond, both of London, Dolberg of Rostock, Pistor & Martin of Berlin.

Artificial Horizon
The sextant and circle are not always used on board ship; they are sometimes used by navigators on shore, and are used by land surveyors and explorers. In these conditions, an artificial horizon is necessary, and this can be provided by a level flat surface.

There are two common forms of the artificial horizon. The older is the trough of wood or iron into which liquid mercury is poured from a stone bottle. The liquid metal gives a highly reflective surface, and naturally forms an absolutely flat surface. To prevent wind ruffling it, the trough is covered by a roof-like triangular box with slanting sides of plate glass. The whole set is packed into a wooden box, and is quite often not recognised for what it is. The same applies to the later form (which is still in production, of course) which consists of a plate of black glass supported by three levelling screws, with a bubble level attached to the plate.

Bubble Sextant
At the end of the nineteenth century, when ballooning had become popular, the bubble sextant was devised. This also had great use after the aeroplane made its first extended flight in 1903. It is a sextant with a bubble level fitted to one limb, so that instead of viewing the horizon, the observer looks at the image of the bubble in a mirror placed at 45° above it. The bubble acts as the horizon marker, an obvious gain for airmen.

Mariner's Compass
The term 'mariner's compass' is usually taken to mean the magnetic compass, but it originally meant the division of the circle of the horizon into 32 points.

The four cardinal points of the compass are North, East, South and West, and the divisions run N., N. by E., NNE., NE. by N., NE. and so on. These are the wind directions, or rhumbs of the wind. Thus, a rhumb-line is the direction followed by a ship sailing on one course, and this can be plotted on a chart. With 32 principal points, the angular distance between two successive points is $11° 15'$, and with suitably constructed charts, it was possible to sail along a rhumb-line by using a compass, and so to simplify the task of the navigator and helmsman. The compass rose (that is, the printed compass card) adopted the earlier wind rose.

Magnetic Compass

The Pole Star, Polaris, was the seaman's lodestar (star that shows the way), and so the magnetic stone that magnetised the needle on the new compass was called a lodestone (also loadstone). The knowledge of the

Trade card of John Browne, Wapping, c. 1750.

direction-finding property of the lodestone came from China in the late twelfth century.

Magnetic compasses, using a single needle and not a card, are found on some sundials of the fifteenth century. By the sixteenth century, the navigator's magnetic compass was a soft iron wire bent to a lozenge shape stuck to the underside of a circular card which was suspended on a pin. The lodestone was necessary to remagnetise the needle as it weakened. In the eighteenth century, Dr. Gowin Knight invented the artificial, compressed powder magnet, and made steel needles for the compass, and his improvement was patented in 1766.

The mariner's compass takes a number of forms. Early ones are in a circular box of wood, then brass takes over. A hanging compass in copper or brass is one that is intended to be hung over the master's bunk and read from underneath. A Portuguese example is dated 1806.

Azimuth Compass

This can be quite large, consisting of a brass case mounted on gimbals which contains the rose, and a sight and string gnomon on the top of the case. The rule attached to the sight can move over a degree scale from $45°-0°-45°$.

This was a popular instrument in the seventeenth and eighteenth centuries, and it was an essential one for determining the deviation of the compass from true North. The magnetic North varies considerably over the globe, and a check has to be made by finding when the Sun is due South, or by finding its bearing at sunrise, when the latitude and the date would also need to be known. Fine, large, azimuth compasses were made by Walter Hayes, Richard Glynne, and J. Fowler, all of London, and by Benjamin Ayres of Amsterdam. Small examples exist, made in about 1800 by Spenser, Browning & Rust, the well-known octant scale dividers.

Binnacle

The binnacle was the place near the helm where the compass was kept, and the name became attached to the cupboard or box with glass lid in which the compass was housed. Sometimes rectangular, those of the later nineteenth and twentieth centuries are cylindrical, and can be four foot high if deck mounted, or much shorter if mounted elsewhere. These binnacles are of mahogany or similar dense wood, with a rounded brass hood containing a glass port to view the compass card. There are also small compartments at each side to contain a lamp. The card is probably to the design of Lord Kelvin, the famous physicist, who in 1873 developed a superior system of very light magnetic needles, grouped parallel to one another, attached to a card rim that carried the points of the compass marked on it. James White, 16 Cambridge Street, Glasgow, was at first the sole maker. When used on iron ships, which have a magnetisation of their own, correctors have to be fitted to the binnacles. These are spheres of iron on each side of the compass case.

Another improvement that is sometimes found is the card floating in liquid; this greatly reduced the wobble in rough seas. It was introduced by E. J. Dent, the chronometer maker, in 1844. As with chronometers and all other navigator's instruments, the retailer's name, not the manufacturer's, is the one usually found. There were retailers in all the major ports.

Logs

Until the sixteenth century, seamen estimated the speed of their ship through the water by experience. Then some threw out an object and timed it passing two fixed points on board, a rough and ready estimate of timing over a measured distance. In the mid-sixteenth century was produced the 'English log', where a log or lump of wood attached to a line was thrown overboard. The length of the line run out in half a minute (measured by a sand-glass), gave the measure of the speed. By tying knots in the line at every seven fathoms, (1 fathom = 6 feet [1.8 m]) a count of the knots streamed out in half a minute gave the way of the ship in miles per hour. It was then taken that 60 miles made one degree on the meridian. This is a crude measure, but any standard is better than none. From the log-line we derive the word 'knot' for the speed of a ship. Nineteenth-century log-lines on their reels, and perhaps their floats, may be found, but they are not common.

Mechanical logs were proposed by several inventors in the eighteenth century, but the first successful recording log was that patented in 1802 by Edward Massey, the Newcastle instrument maker. These logs depend on rotors, and registering dials.

The 'Dutch log' uses the old-fashioned method of timing a piece of wood past a measured distance on the ship's side. This technique was employed by Dutch seamen from the seventeenth to the nineteenth century, and the 'aid' is in the form of a brass tobacco box, rectangular in form, with rounded ends. There is usually a perpetual calendar and two engraved figures on the lid, and underneath are engraved the speed tables that convert the time measured into speed.

Traverse Board

The helmsman's traverse board was used to plot the course taken by the ship which had to progress by a series of tacks into the wind. Pegs are attached to the board by string, and these are pushed into holes indicating the compass bearing, and into holes indicating the time steered on that bearing. The time was measured by a sand-glass in half hours. At the end of the watch, the mean course and distance sailed could be worked out. The speed through the water would also need to be known, and this was taken by the log-line and charted by pegs in the rectangular part of the board.

The helmsman's traverse board is mentioned in 1528 as part of the navigator's set of necessary instruments. It continued in use in coasting vessels in northern waters well into the nineteenth century. Made of wood, and measuring about 12×8 inches (30×20 cm), these objects were part of the ship's equipment that would not be thought important to keep when the ship was broken up. Few have survived, and these are nineteenth-century, although dating is difficult. The possibility of faking is also very great.

Marine Chronometer

The problem of finding the longitude at sea was solved in principle though not in practice by the sixteenth century. Two rival methods were discussed, the keeping of the time at the port of departure by a clock, and the measurement of the angular distance of the Moon against certain prominent stars compared against a set of standard tables. This method became known as the 'lunar distance' method, and was to be accomplished by using a cross-staff. The technology was not sufficiently advanced until the mid-eighteenth century for this method to be of use, and even then it depended on long calculations, and on clear sightings of the Moon and stars.

The other method of finding longitude by using a clock, and comparing its time with a measurement of the local time at the ship's position, also depended on technological advance. The first possible clockwork mechanism, a triumph of applied physics, was John Harrison's marine chronometer of 1735. He made two more of these large clocks, designed to be independent of the ship's motion and of temperature changes, in 1737 and 1757, and, finally, a fourth in the form of a large pocket watch, $5\frac{1}{4}$-inch (13.5 cm) diameter, in 1759. It was this chronometer that set the pattern for all subsequent ships' clocks. These beautiful mechanisms may be seen working in the Navigation Gallery of the National Maritime

Museum, Greenwich.

John Arnold and Son, Thomas Mudge Senior, and Junior, were early names in chronometer making. By the 1790s, the East India Company were using these new navigational aids, and Royal Navy officers would buy their own. The breakthrough in quantity production came in the late 1790s. By 1820, two firms, John Arnold and Thomas Earnshaw, had produced over 2,000 chronometers, and another English firm, Barraud, produced about 1,000. The only competition came from France, where Le Roy was a pioneer, and was followed by Berthoud.

The industry, which was a craft of individuals, not a factory-based one, was very active until about 1840 to satisfy the market for chronometers, but then the demand slackened because the instruments were so well-made that they did not wear out—some are even perfectly satisfactory today. In 1840, the firms of Arnold and Dent were producing 60 box chronometers a year which sold for around £40.

From the 1850s and well into the twentieth century, the two dominant English firms were Thomas Mercer and Victor Kullberg. It is not generally realised that these firms produced virtually the whole supply of marine chronometers for the English market and for a considerable part of the foreign market. For example, Kullberg would sell a chronometer to Frodsham & Keen of Liverpool for £25; it was then retailed for £38, with, of course, the retailer's name on the dial. Similarly, the name on a Mercer instrument was often that of the retailer, and this applies to foreign as well as English retailers. Again, a chronometer of about 1840 signed by John Arnold of London, has the retailer's label in the lid—Peter Walther of Baltimore, United States. Although the maker's name and serial number may be found on the movement, these were sometimes changed, so there is no absolute guide unless a firm's register book survives.

Other, smaller firms in England by the end of the nineteenth century were Johannson, Usher & Cole, and Dents. In France, real makers were Le Roy and Nardin, although their output was small. It is estimated that in 1889 the total output of British firms was 300 a year, whereas in France it was 40.

Early chronometers were placed in eight-sided mahogany cases, with a glass top. From about 1800, however, the form was a rectangular box, with brass binding, and a glass top. The instrument is mounted on gimbals. The mechanism is a masterpiece of craftsmanship, but it needs considerable study to understand the intricacies of the workings.

The National Maritime Museum, Greenwich, keeps a register of chronometers. This is important, because the design is constant, and some may be older than one would think, and others much more recent, from the 1930s perhaps. In 1978, late nineteenth and early twentieth century examples were being sold for about £500, although earlier ones with a famous name would cost far more.

Dip Circle

Another magnetic device is the dip circle, or dipping needle. This is a magnetic needle that moves in a vertical plane, whereas in the compass it moves in a horizontal plane. The dip circle measures the vertical component of the earth's magnetic field. The Elizabethan navigator and instrument maker, Robert Norman, discovered the effect of dip in about 1576, and he invented the dipping needle. At that time it was thought that the angle of dip could find the latitude more easily than by other means, but this proved not to be true. The dip circles that may be found today are not navigators' equipment, but that of scientific explorers, who need to study the way the earth's magnetic field varies from place to place. Captain Cook took with him on his second voyage a dip circle made in 1772 by Edward Nairne, then one of the foremost of London's scientific instrument makers. Dollond, Troughton and other makers were producing dip circles at the end of the eighteenth century.

3
Surveying Instruments

Wandering tribal peoples do not need to survey land; it is not until settled, agricultural communities develop that the division of land into definable plots becomes important. At first, the boundaries have to be fixed to mark agreed division between neighbours; then the areas, location and value are necessary for taxation and for property rights. Archaeologists have shown that some form of surveying existed in the river valleys of the Tigris and Euphrates, and of the Nile, before 1000 B.C. The instruments seem to have been inexact, composed as they were of cords, rods, and simple sighting devices.

The earliest book known to have been written on surveying is by Hero of Alexandria, a Greek engineer and scientist who flourished in about A.D. 100. His book, *Treatise on the Dioptra*, gives the basic principles of the art of surveying, and describes a levelling instrument, the dioptra. The Romans used a similar instrument, a T-shape with open sights and a plumb bob, and also a level consisting of a long, shallow trough filled with water. Water, of course, always gives an exactly horizontal surface.

Roman techniques continued to be used until about 1500, when increased wealth and an enlarged population caused the profession of surveyor to grow. In England, following the dissolution of the monasteries by Henry VIII in 1539, the new owners favoured by the king needed to have their land demarcated. Doubtless it was this activity that encouraged Leonard Digges, a graduate of Oxford University, to invent a form of theodolite, consisting of a horizontal circle divided into 360 degrees, with a semi-circle at right angles above it that could measure angles of elevation. His design was published in 1556, and there are two theodolites in existence, made in London by Humphrey Cole, bearing the dates 1574 and 1586, that put into practice the design of Digges. A superb theodolite was constructed in about 1600 by Erasmus Habermel, the Prague instrument maker retained by the Emperor Rudolf II. But it seems that Digges was not the first to think of putting a vertical circle above a horizontal one—in effect two astrolabes, suitably mounted and modified. The German, Waldseemüller, had his invention illustrated in a book published in 1512.

An entirely new instrument, of considerable importance both practically and scientifically, was the magnetic compass that is known to have been in use in China during the eleventh century for cartographic surveys. To Alexander Neckham we owe the earliest reference to the compass for navigation in his *De Naturis Rerum* (1180). The magnetic compass became established at sea long before it was accepted on land. However, by the early sixteenth century, an astrolabe had been made incorporating a compass, and it was added to the circumferentor, which was an angle-measuring instrument, a development from the astrolabe used horizontally and not in its normal position. The compass was incorporated as a matter of course in the later sixteenth-century theodolites.

The compass needle points to magnetic North, and not to the geographic North Pole. The difference is known as the declination (or deviation) of the magnetic needle, and its value depends on the location and on the year. At London, the needle can move through $35°$ in 240 years as shown in the Table. A knowledge of magnetic declination can assist in dating, when it is marked on a compass or on a sundial as it often is. In 1979 for the British Isles, the average annual decrease in declination was $6\frac{1}{2}$ minutes of arc.

Levels

Levelling is the art of finding a line parallel to the horizon at one or more stations, to discover how much one plane is higher than another, a particularly important skill when cutting canals. For this last purpose, great accuracy is necessary, and allowance has to be made for the curvature of the Earth. For building work, simple levels will be adequate.

Erasmus Habermel of Prague, in about 1600, included with a set of beautifully made surveying instruments a water level. But for convenience, a spirit level consisting of a long glass tube containing coloured spirits of wine was preferable. An early eighteenth-century example exists which is set in mahogany and is about two feet (60 cm) in length. Simple spirit levels with a pair of sights, fitting on a staff, were called drainage levels in the nineteenth century. Even with telescopic sights, a bubble tube is essential, and theodolites carry a pair of levels set at right angles to each other.

The oldest form of the modern surveyor's level was devised by Jonathan Sisson, a renowned mathematical instrument maker working in London during the second quarter of the eighteenth century. The

Table to show magnetic declination near London

Date	Declination	Date	Declination West	Date	Declination West
1580	11° 15′ E	1817	24° 36′	1871	20° 10′
1622	6° 00′ E	1818	24° 38′	1872	20° 00′
1634	4° 06′ E	1819	24° 36′	1873	19° 58′
1657	0° 00′	1820	24° 34′	1874	19° 52′
1665	1° 22′ W	1858	21° 54′	1875	19° 41′
1672	2° 30′ W	1859	21° 47′	1876	19° 32′
1692	6° 00′ W	1860	21° 40′	1877	19° 22′
1723	14° 17′ W	1861	21° 32′	1878	19° 14′
1748	17° 40′ W	1862	21° 23′	1879	19° 06′
1773	21° 09′ W	1863	21° 13′	1880	18° 57′
1787	23° 19′ W	1864	21° 03′	1881	18° 50′
1795	23° 57′ W	1865	20° 59′	1882	18° 45′
1802	24° 06′ W	1866	20° 51′	1883	18° 40′
1805	24° 08′ W	1867	20° 40′	1884	18° 32′
1806	24° 15′ W	1868	20° 33′	1885	18° 25′
1809	24° 22′ W	1869	20° 26′	1900	16° 52′
1812	24° 28′ W	1870	20° 19′	1910	16° 03′

pattern is known as the Y-level, because the telescope is supported in Y-shaped bearings, with brass straps over the top to hold the tube tight, allowing the telescope to be reversed to check the setting. Below the telescope is the bubble tube, and in the base, above the fixing at the head of the tripod, is a large magnetic compass.

Improvements were made to the level by Jesse Ramsden, who did so much for all precision instruments in the last quarter of the eighteenth century. A hundred years later, the Y-level was no longer popular in Britain, but continued in use on the continent and in America. Although an excellent instrument, it had too many adjustments for use in difficult terrain such as is found in Africa and India.

The instrument that superseded the Y-level was the dumpy-level, in which the telescope could be fixed, because lenses were accurately centred by the 1840s. The civil engineer, William Gravatt, produced

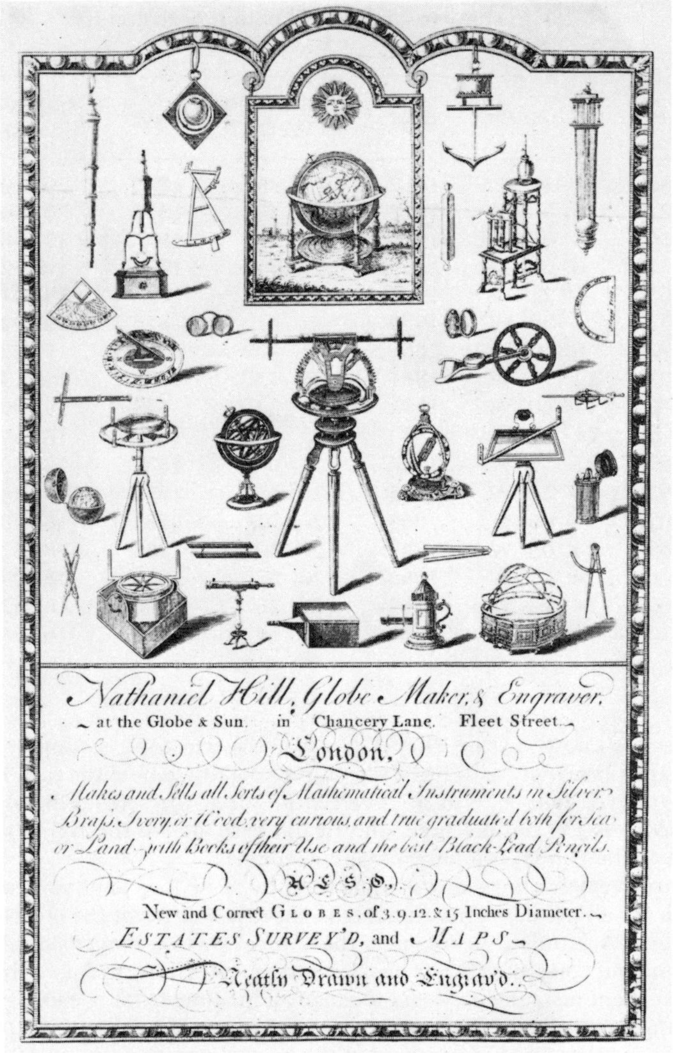

Trade card of Nathaniel Hill, Chancery Lane, 1746–66.

his design for the dumpy for use during the railway mania of 1848. It was compact, robust, and had a large objective lens in the telescope, and a cross bubble in addition to the bubble tube on the telescope. The Y had a telescope about 20 inches (50 cm) or more in length; the dumpy had one 12 inches (30 cm) long.

Levelling Staff

A level is used in conjunction with a levelling staff, which is usually a rectangular wooden tube with two further sections that telescope into the outer one. Closed, the length is about $5\frac{1}{2}$ feet (1.65 m), open, 14 feet (4.2 m). One face is marked out in feet and tenths, the foot marks in red, the tenths in black. A popular type was that invented by Thomas Sopwith in 1838, but surveyors tended to commission their own designs, so among those found today there are many variations.

Barometer

For measuring great altitudes in mountains, where the ordinary operations of levelling are impossible, the barometer was used. The air pressure varies with height and with temperature, so it is possible to work out altitudes on mountains, or in air-balloons, with a barometer and thermometer. In about 1800, 'mountain barometers' were made and sold by W & S Jones of Holborn, London. Such barometric measurements were greatly improved after the invention, in 1845, of the aneroid ('without fluid') barometer by Lucien Vidie of Paris (see Chapter 6). Pocket aneroids, the size of a watch, were made from 1860 by Negretti & Zambra of London, and were capable of measuring heights of up to 20,000 feet (c. 6,000 m). A temperature-compensated, surveyor's aneroid, $4\frac{1}{2}$ inches (11.5 cm) in diameter, was sold in around 1900 by W. F. Stanley & Co., for altitudes and depths of mines, that was claimed to give results accurate to one yard (90 cm).

Theodolite

As has already been remarked, the theodolite was invented in the mid-sixteenth century, but it was not developed significantly until the eighteenth century. Jonathan Sisson's first theodolites were traditional, with plain sights, but he made the important step of substituting a telescopic sight. Jesse Ramsden greatly improved degree-scale division so that by 1800 the instrument was virtually in its final form. It is regarded as the most important of the surveying instruments, as it can measure at the same time both the horizontal angles between two points and their angle of elevation. It consists of a horizontal divided circle (the diameter of which gives the size of the instrument, e.g. 6-inch [15-cm]), probably with small microscopes to read the verniers; a compass; perhaps a fixed telescope (not always fitted) below the compass; a semi-circular divided arc with the curve uppermost on earlier instruments, and downwards on later ones, surmounted by a telescope with bubble tube, as on a surveyor's level. A transit theodolite has a complete 360° vertical circle. Naturally, the nineteenth century, with the great surveys of America, Africa and India, and railway construction in all parts of the world, saw a great many variations in constructional detail of the instrument, and special adaptations for such things as laying out railway curves.

From the time when the Enclosure Acts brought large areas of land under cultivation by private land owners, throughout the Industrial Revolution, with its road, canal, and railway building, and the extension of similar projects into the vast areas of the Empire, the demand for surveying instruments of all kinds on the British market was enormous. Therefore it is not surprising that levels, theodolites and other surveying precision instruments were made by the first rank of English makers. Sisson and Ramsden have already been mentioned, and one should add George Adams, Thomas Jones, William Cary, Dollond, Edward Troughton (after 1826, Troughton & Sims), Negretti & Zambra, Elliott Brothers, J. H. Steward, W. F. Stanley, T. Cooke & Sons, York (after 1922, Cooke, Troughton & Simms Ltd.). Continental makers of standing were F. W. Breithaupt & Sohn, Cassel (awarded a prize medal at the 1851 Great Exhibition); Claude Langlois (flourished 1730–50) and Etienne Lenoir (flourished 1780–1830) of Paris; Beaulieu of Belgium (another 1851 prize medallist); W. Schenck & Co. of Berne.

Graphometer

This came to be regarded in the late nineteenth century as satisfying the need for a simple, strong, portable, but inexpensive and accurate instrument for preliminary surveys. It could work in the horizontal and vertical planes. It was invented by Philippe Danfrie of Paris in about 1597, and his instrument consisted of two alidades, or sighting rules, one fixed to a semi-circle divided in degrees, and the other movable over the scale of degrees. The whole was mounted on a tripod by means of a ball and socket joint. A magnetic compass was usually included.

The graphometer was more popular on the continent of Europe, particularly in France, than in Britain, although English-made instruments are to be found. Examples are signed by P. Danfrie, Vernier (1630),

Pierre Sevin (1665), Choizy (1667), and the eighteenth-century makers N. Bion, Chapotot, Maquart and Langlois.

Circumferentor

A graphometer can be made with a full circle rather than a semi-circle, and so may become confused with the circumferentor. The original form of theodolite, as devised by Digges, used open sights which were in the course of time replaced by telescopic sights. The compass box over the axis was made longer, and the superstructure was removed so that the needle could be read accurately by placing the eye directly above it; but the two pairs of horizontal sights were retained. These modifications produced the circumferentor from the old form of theodolite, existing alongside the telescopic theodolite. By the end of the eighteenth century, the circumferentor consisted of a pair of sights on the North-South axis of a large compass, of which the South end of the needle took the bearings. This means that the compass rose is divided in the contrary way to the usual, East being where you would expect to find West. Thus, if you sight to the S.E., the needle has to settle to give a reading of 45° S.E., which would actually read S.W. on a normal compass rose. By the early nineteenth century, theodolites were so improved that the circumferentor along with the graphometer went out of favour in Europe; but it remained important for taking surveys through woods and uncleared ground, as in America. It was also used in coal mines, and the term 'circumferentor' became an alternative to miner's compass. Here a large compass is specially important, because it may be the only way angles can be taken in low and tortuous mine tunnels. The compass is on a bar with folding sights at each end, and a pair of spirit levels.

Circumferentors were made in Italy, France, Holland and England. Those dating from the eighteenth century may bear the names John Worgan, Thomas Heath, John Bennett, George Adams, all of London; and Butterfield in Paris. Mining compasses were made by W & S Jones, Dollond, William Cary, Negretti & Zambra and William Stanley. Provincial retailers' names are also found on standard products from London makers, or instruments imported from Paris.

Plane-table

Surveying by the plane-table (before 1830, plain-table) is quite rapid, as every angle taken in the field is plotted directly, every distance is plotted to scale at the time, and all distances are laid off by scale and compasses. The table is of a smooth board, of beech or mahogany, measuring about 20 × 15 inches (50 × 37 cm), with an outer edging that can fit over the board rather like the frame of a picture. This frame holds down a large sheet of paper placed over the board, and keeps it taut. Underneath is a brass socket which fits on to the top of a wooden tripod. On one side projects a magnetic compass box. On the top of the board is placed the alidade (index, or sighting rule), a sort of brass ruler, about 20 inches (50 cm) long, with one edge chamfered. At each end is a brass, slit sight, and engraved on the upper side of the rule are a few scales (perhaps 1:10, 1:50, 1:100) for plotting ground measurements with the aid of a pair of compasses.

In use, the table is positioned so that the magnetic needle is due North, and then the index is used to sight various features, and their distances are measured; consequently, angles are drawn directly from the edge of the index, and distances are drawn to scale. By removing the table to other sites, a complete survey of a small region can be made in one step. Rainy weather would be a grave disadvantage, but was predictable, and therefore avoidable in India where very large areas were covered using plane-tables in the late nineteenth century.

The plane-table was first referred to in English by Cyprian Lucar in 1590, in a text that described surveying by the use of the table only, and it continued in use up to the twentieth century. Nearly all mathematical instrument makers offered plane-tables for sale, but they could also be made up by any carpenter, and the compass could be bought from a ships' chandler, or elsewhere. They are rather rare as collectors' items, since, being made of wood, they may have decayed, or been thought of little value. Examples from the eighteenth century that are in collections bear the names of George Adams, Senior or Junior, of London, and Langlois of Paris.

Gunter's Chain

This is used for measuring length on the ground. It is made of iron, so that it will keep its length, which a cloth tape will not. There are 100 links in a chain, the length of which is 22 yards (c. 20 m). The chain was developed in 1620 by Edmund Gunter, who was professor of astronomy at Gresham College, London. He was in favour of decimalisation, and a square chain is one tenth of an acre (1 acre = 4840 sq. yards). The chain is, however, based on a much older measure, the rod, pole, or perch (names given to the same thing in different parts of Britain), which was $16\frac{1}{2}$ feet (c. 5 m) in length, or one quarter of a chain. Ten chains equal

1 furlong, which is one eighth of a mile. Each tenth link is marked by a piece of brass notched for identification. By the mid-nineteenth century, there were other chains in use, including 100-foot (30 m), used in North America, 50-foot (15 m), and 20-metre with centimetre links. The product of wrought-iron smiths, the surveyor's chain is difficult to date unless there happens to be a maker's mark recorded somewhere.

Cross-staff
The cross-staff used by the surveyor must not be confused with the seaman's cross-staff, or fore-staff (see Chapter 2). The surveyor uses a brass, or boxwood, cross sight on the top of a pole, the sightlines being exactly 90° to each other. It is used with a chain to measure 'off-sets'. When running out a chain in a straight line, features on either side, such as a tree, river bend, or a building, can be drawn on the plan quite readily by measuring the distance from the chain line to the feature when the distance is taken exactly 90° from the chain. The cross-staff enables this to be done with some accuracy, and a simple and cheap survey can thus be made.

Optical Square
The principle is an old one, but the compact cross-staff dates from the eighteenth century, and was used by surveyors all over Europe. An improvement introduced in the nineteenth century is the optical square, where a half-silvered mirror at 45°, set in a small drum-shaped brass box, enables the surveyor to see the end of the chain line and the feature at right angles superimposed in the mirror, giving a more accurate starting point for the off-set. Sometimes the instrument is to be found with two pairs of cross sights, so making the case octagonal, and a magnetic compass may be fitted at the top. Examples found today are likely to be from the later nineteenth and early twentieth centuries, and may bear the name W. F. Stanley.

Surveyor's Wheel
The surveyor's wheel goes by several different names; in the eighteenth century it was generally known as a 'waywiser', and in the late nineteenth century as a 'perambulator'; it is also referred to as an 'hodometer', from the Greek, 'way measure' (but see over). A type of instrument dating from Roman times, it was re-introduced in the seventeenth century, and is used for measuring roads. On pavements and asphalt roads it is reasonably accurate, and is more useful than a chain in condi-

tions of traffic. The outer rim, or tyre, may measure 36, 72, or 100 inches (90, 180 or 250 cm), giving wheel diameters of about $11\frac{3}{4}$, 23, and 32 inches (29.5, 59 and 82 cm) respectively. The revolutions of the wheel are (29.5, 59 and 82 cm) respectively. The revolutions of the wheel are recorded on a large dial mounted in a box, either adjacent to the axle or below the handle. The dial with two hands records yards, poles, furlongs and miles. The frame is nearly always of mahogany, and the tyre of iron or hard brass.

Obviously made by specialists, probably makers of coach wheels, the signatures of the usual instrument makers are found engraved on the dial plates, for it was they who sold waywisers. London tradesmen include Heath, Heath & Wing, Martin, Adams, Dollond, Cary, W & S Jones. Late nineteenth- and twentieth-century versions employ bicycle-type wheels, W. F. Stanley being a typical maker.

Hodometer

An associated instrument is the hodometer (also written odometer) which was fixed to a carriage wheel to record distance travelled. German and Dutch versions usually have three separate dials to record the measures.

Pedometer

This is a similar instrument to the hodometer, used to find out roughly the distance covered while walking. It was patented in 1831 by William Payne, and has the appearance of a watch with a single hand. The dial is normally marked 1 to 12 like a watch, so it may at first sight be confused with a timepiece. Inside, a weighted arm on a ratchet clicks up each step.

Pocket Sextant

The pocket sextant is an extremely compact instrument devised by Edward Troughton in about 1800. It is also called a box sextant, and in its early years was known as a snuff box sextant, because of its size— only $2\frac{1}{2}$ or 3 inches (6.5 or 8 cm) in diameter, and 2 inches (5 cm) deep. It was a great improvement on the cross-staff for setting $90°$ exactly, as, with a half-silvered mirror, the images of the chosen two points are made to coincide. Surveyors came to regard the pocket sextant as essential for use in trigonometrical observations, as any angle in the vertical or horizontal can be taken. A professional man wrote in 1888, 'This is an instrument, without which no surveyor should go into the field.'

The small size compared with the seaman's sextant (see Chapter 2) was facilitated by the greatly refined circle-dividing techniques brought into use by Jesse Ramsden, and improved by Edward Troughton. His tiny scales had to be read through a small magnifying glass.

Prismatic Compass

Another instrument regarded in the nineteenth century as essential equipment for the surveyor was the prismatic compass; since it could take bearings, and be used in traversing, it was the only reliable means of determining magnetic North in the absence of a theodolite. Compasses have been included as part of surveying equipment since the sixteenth century, and pocket compasses, varying in size from 2 to 6 inches (5 to 15 cm), have been separate instruments from that time to this. The first compass with some accuracy—readable to a third of a degree—was the prismatic. The name refers to a right-angled prism attached to the back-sight that can be positioned over the rim of the compass card so that the degrees can be read while sighting the point of observation. The card is divided into 360°, which figure has to be inscribed on the South point, because that is where the eye and prism are positioned when looking due North. Also, the figures have to be printed in reverse, because of the reflection in the prism.

The prismatic compass was invented, and patented, in 1812 by Charles Augustus Schmalcalder, a mathematical instrument maker in the Strand, London. At the end of the patent, other makers copied the design, for example, Troughton & Simms, and Cary, and it became established as an essential instrument for walkers, explorers, army officers, and many others.

Clinometer

Sometimes the prismatic compass would incorporate in its brass case a clinometer, which measures vertical angles by means of a weighted wheel. This keeps its position while the case to which the sights are fixed is turned so that the point of observation is seen in the sights. The angle is read through the prism attached to the backsight. A clinometer scale is marked as well, giving the rise or fall in terms of inches per yard.

Another small, handy clinometer is the Abney level, named after Captain William Abney of the School of Military Engineering, Chatham. A small telescope is in a rectangular tube which has attached to it a semi-circle divided into degrees and a clinometer scale. At the centre of the arc is a pivot with a bubble tube. The bubble can be seen through a hole in the telescope tube, via a mirror, so that the point sighted and the level bubble are seen together. The angle through which the pivot has been turned is read off the scale.

Clinometer Rule

A simpler instrument is the clinometer rule, 6 inches (15 cm) long, of boxwood and brass, jointed like a carpenter's rule, with a small 90° quadrant at the join. Each arm has a bubble tube, and the top arm a pair of sights. An inclination table is inscribed on one arm, and sometimes a magnetic compass is incorporated. This is a useful instrument for geologists.

4
Drawing and Calculating Instruments

Surveyors, astronomers, navigators, architects, engineers and draughtsmen, in short all scientific and technical practitioners, have certain tools of the trade in common. All need to draw accurately, whether it is land boundaries on a map, coordinates on a star chart or the design for a steam engine, and all need to calculate, which in the present context means addition, subtraction, multiplication, and to use trigonometrical functions: basic stuff but tedious and time-consuming if done the long way with pencil and paper. To meet these demands, there evolved drawing instruments and calculating instruments.

Sets of Drawing Instruments
Drawing involves ruling a straight line, parallel lines, and lines at a given angle to another, as well as measuring parts of lines. For these purposes there are rulers, parallel rules that can extend to a required distance and protractors. Measurements are normally to scale, for example, 1 inch may represent 1 mile on the ground (a scale of 1:63,360), or a special scale is cut so that there are 4 chains to 1 inch (20 inches to 1 mile). A typical set of drawing instruments includes ruler and scale; parallel rulers; circular or semi-circular protractor; plotting scales and rectangular protractor combined; a pair of compasses for drawing circles; spring bows for small circles; a pair of dividers for pricking off lengths; pens, pencils, and similar attachments for the legs of the compasses. Sets may be extended by additional sizes of compasses and dividers, and some other instruments, such as a sector (see page 58).

Drawing instruments are produced in two main qualities, one for learners and one for professionals. This distinction becomes more important during the nineteenth century when more technical colleges were founded and schools became more technically minded. The presentation of the sets varies; in the eighteenth century they were commonly in black, fishskin covered cases, with flip-top lids, but could be in hinged boxes, perhaps rather ornate. In the nineteenth century the range of boxes was much extended. By the end of the century, the cases for professionals could be in mahogany or rosewood with brass-bound corners, and with one or more lift-out trays, lined with velvet, usually dyed blue. Flat leather-covered cases, with rounded corners and a bolt fastening, were made in France for carrying in the pocket, and were imported and then copied by the British trade.

Compasses and dividers are generally of brass with steel points of triangular cross-section. The rulers and scales are of boxwood for cheapness, or brass, ivory, or occasionally of silver. Parallel rulers are of ebony, ivory or brass. In about 1880, Negretti & Zambra were supplying sets of mathematical drawing instruments made in German silver (a copper, zinc, and nickel alloy) as being best suited for use in warm, damp climates where brass would quickly corrode. Large sets could include colours, palettes and brushes.

Additional instruments, commonly sold separately from the sets, include beam compass for large circles; three-legged or triangular compasses; elliptical trammel, and ellipsograph for drawing ellipses; proportional compasses for taking ratios (see below); rolling parallel rulers; circular protractors with hinged, folding side arms with pricking points, tangent screw, and vernier; set squares; sets of architectural and other curves, to provide a variety of ruling edges; jointed measuring rules; and, of course, a T-square and drawing board.

Draughting instruments are very ancient in origin; compasses and dividers can be traced to Babylonian times; Leonardo da Vinci, at the end of the fifteenth century, sketched drawing pens and proportional compasses. In some museums there are superb examples of sets of drawing instruments made for courtly presentation by Italian and French craftsmen of the sixteenth and seventeenth centuries, with elaborately formed and decorated instruments in gilt copper or brass, placed in tooled leather cases. Such pieces are naturally very rare, and command very high prices today.

Proportional Compass
The proportional compass is used to enlarge or reduce a drawing by having two arms and a pivot part way along, so that the ends open out to different lengths, usually in the ratio 2:1. It was known to the Victorians as a 'whole and half compass'. The Swiss instrument-maker, Jost Bürgi, in about 1600, made the instrument with a slot in each arm and a movable pivot, so that the ratio could be varied at will. The posi-

tions for certain ratios were marked: scale of lines for lengths; scale of circles to divide the circumference into any number of equal parts; scale of planes for areas; scale of solids for volumes. The instrument is still made and sold today. (See also Sectors, p. 58.)

Pantograph
Change of scale is frequently required by draughtsmen, and to speed things up other new instruments were developed, in particular the pantograph, which was invented between 1603 and 1605 by the German astronomer, Christoph Scheiner, and greatly improved in 1743 by the Parisian craftsman, Claude Langlois. The railway building of the nineteenth century ensured a need for this device. It consists of four brass bars, jointed in pairs, one pair being twice the length of the other. Under the joints are small castors, and one long bar has a tracing point, and a short arm has a pen held by a sliding head that is set to the ratio required. On the other long bar is a pivot point in the form of a heavy brass disc.

Eidograph
The eidograph, an improved instrument for reducing or enlarging drawings, was invented in 1801 by William Wallace, who subsequently became professor of mathematics at the University of Edinburgh. Although similar to the pantograph, any ratio could be taken between the limits of one to three, for example, 9:25.

Polar Planimeter
Areas on maps and plans have to be measured, and one laborious way is to place over the area a sheet of thin paper with a grid of small squares which have to be counted. The polar planimeter measures areas merely by tracing the outline. It consists of two arms, one with a pin to fix it to the board, and the other with a tracing point. At the joint is a small wheel that rotates as the tracing movement is performed, and the area is read off a dial. This ingenious instrument was the invention, in 1854, of Jakob Amsler, professor of mathematics at the University of Schaffhausen in Switzerland.

Opisometer, Chartometer
The opisometer is a small device for measuring the lengths of roads, rivers, walls, etc., on maps. It is simply a milled wheel on a screw thread with a handle. The wheel traces the route, and is then wound back-

wards on the scale at the edge of the map. The chartometer is the same thing but with a dial and pointer to give the measure immediately.

Station Pointer

For surveying in new regions, and especially for hydrographic surveys, the station pointer is essential. It is a kind of double-arm protractor, where two angles relative to a base may be laid off at the same time. For taking coastal soundings, the angles between three points on land are measured with a sextant, the two movable arms are set relative to the fixed arm and the instrument is placed over the chart. When the arms all match the features on the shore, the boat's position is fixed exactly, and the point is pricked onto the chart. The diameter of the protractor varies between 5 and 12 inches (12–30 cm), and the arms are 12 to 15 inches (30–37 cm) long, with brass or wooden extension pieces. This instrument was the invention of the Admiralty Surveyor, Murdoch Mackenzie, who in 1774 published details in his book *Treatise on Maritime Surveying*.

Sectors

Sectors were made with a variety of scales for use in calculation by navigators, surveyors, gunners, and draughtsmen, and at first sight they look like a jointed rule, and are usually made of ivory, brass, wood, or sometimes silver. The sector was in use in England by 1597 for gunnery, and Thomas Hood's design was made in brass with an arc of 150° and two arms which carried scales of proportion based on the principle of similar triangles. These scales were used in conjunction with a pair of dividers—a necessary accompanying instrument for all types of sector.

Galileo developed a sector between 1597 and 1599 for use as a general-purpose calculator, and he called it a compass, and on the Continent it became known as the proportional compass. This has caused much confusion, because in Britain the proportional compass is quite a different instrument (see page 56). The European names for the sector are (German) Kreissektor; (Italian) compasso di proporzione; (French) compas de proportion. The proportional compass is known as (German) Proportionalzirkel; (Italian) compasso di riduzione; (French) compas de réduction.

Sectors were in general use for 300 years, but by 1866, W. F. Stanley, the instrument maker, could write, 'The sector is a kind of twofold rule, commonly supplied with a case of mathematical instruments, as a kind of established ornament'.

The sector is engraved with a number of scales of mathematical functions, and it can give similar information to that provided by a slide rule. French sectors differ slightly from English, having fewer scales, being intended for gunnery. The English instrument is essentially a draughtsman's aid. The English sector of the eighteenth or nineteenth century has, in general, the following scales.

L	line of equal parts, 0–10
C	line of chords, 0–60°, used to protract an angle
S or Si	line of sines, 0–90°
T	line of tangents, 0–45°
t	line of tangents to a smaller radius, 45°–75°
S or Se	line of secants, 10°–75°
P or POL	line of polygons, 12–4, for inscribing a regular polygon inside a circle of a given radius

Some other scales may be engraved along the edges:

N or Num	line of numbers, 0–10 twice, used with a pair of dividers in the same manner as a slide rule for multiplication; it is Gunter's scale
R or Rh	line of rhumbs, 0–8, used for plotting a ship's course upon a chart; the scale is in points of the compass, where 32 is a complete circle
Lon	longitude, 60°–0, used in navigation
La	latitude, 0–90° ⎫
Ho	hours, 0–VI ⎭ used in the construction of sundials

The French sector commonly has the following scales:

line of equal parts
line of chords
line of planes (areas)
line of solids (volumes)
calibre of pieces (size of gun barrels)
weight of shot
line of metals (six metals denoted by symbols—gold, lead, silver, copper, iron, tin), used for weight/volume measurements
polygons, 12–3

The use of these scales is unfamiliar to the twentieth century: a good account can be found in Edmund Stone's translation of N. Bion, *Mathematical Instruments* (1758), reprinted in 1972.

Abacus

The history of the abacus runs from the prehistoric era to modern times. The Greek, and later the Roman, abacus was no more than a convenient, flat surface on which pebbles could be placed. The word in Greek means a disc or table. The Latin phrase for reckoning up accounts was 'ponere calculos' which means 'to place the pebbles'. From the word for pebbles derives our words 'calculate', and 'calculus', a branch of mathematics.

The Roman calculating board was divided into columns, headed with the letters which were used to designate numbers: M (1000), C (100), X (10), I (1). Into each section could be placed anything between 1 and 9 pebbles. But it is difficult to add up 8 or 9 pebbles at a glance, so the intermediate numbers, 5, 50, 500, were represented by 1 pebble placed on the line dividing two sections. These were designated V (5), L (50), and D (500). This meant that calculations could be worked with 1 pebble representing 5, and 4 singles.

The way in which the Roman calculating board was used is shown in contemporary illustrations, and the counting pebbles have been discovered on archaeological sites. There also exist a small number of portable bead calculators dating from the Roman period, which are now in museums in London, Paris, and Rome. These devices are small enough to hold in one hand, and consist of beads that are moved in vertical slots. The slots are divided into two sections horizontally; in the upper section is 1 bead for 5; in the lower, 4 beads to be used as singles.

So both the calculating board and the bead abacus existed in Roman times, and both continued in use for many centuries. In Europe, the board with counters was used by government departments and in commerce, and eventually had an interesting side-product in the game of shove-halfpenny, which must have started to pass an idle hour in the counting house, and is still popular in pubs. Counting boards are rarely found on the market, but the counters, known as jettons (French, 'jetons') can occur. These were first imported to Britain from France in the thirteenth century, and from the sixteenth to the eighteenth were produced for use throughout Europe by craftsmen in Nuremberg. These tokens are made of brass, and usually have the head of the reigning monarch on one side and the name of the maker on the other.

The Roman bead calculator developed into the bead-frame abacus which is still used in China, Japan, Russia, and Poland. A rectangular frame is set with parallel rods or wires, on which beads slide up and down. Chinese abacuses have rounded beads on bamboo rods, 2 in the upper section, 5 in the lower. Japanese examples, which first became

1 Armillary Sphere. French, early 19th-century. Printed paper on wood.

2 Astrolabe. English, *c.* 1370. Discovered at Painswick, Gloucestershire. Similar to astrolabe described by Chaucer in 1391.

3 Astrolabe. Persian, *c.* 1710, made by 'Abd al-A'imma.

4 **Sand-glasses.** English, 18th-, or early 19th-century. Left to right: ½ hour; 1 hour (from a church); ¼ hour; 1 hour.

5 **Quadrant.** English, 1658, signed *Henricus Sutton Londini fecit*. Printed paper on oak.

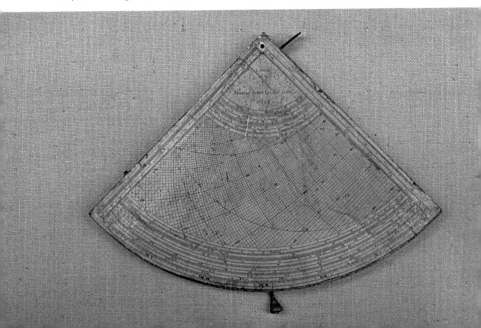

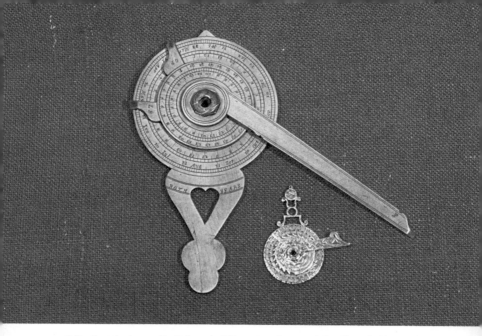

6 Nocturnals. Large: English, early 18th-century, boxwood. Small: probably a replica of a German 17th-century instrument, brass.

7 Sundials. Left to right: Bloud, Dieppe, *c.* 1670; Magnetic Compass, London, *c.* 1825; Polyhedral, Augsburg, *c.* 1780; Butterfield, Paris, *c.* 1700; Equatorial, Augsburg, *c.* 1800.

8 Universal Ring Dial. English, *c.* 1720, signed *I. Coggs fecit.*

9 Planetarium (Grand Orrery). English, *c. 1770*, signed *Geo. Adams, Instrum. Maker to His Majesty, No. 60 Fleet Street, London.*

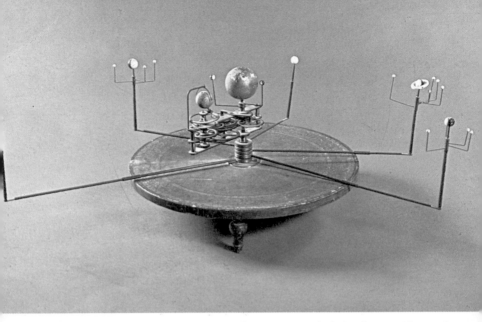

10 Planetarium with Tellurium. English, mid 19th-century. Includes Neptune (discovered 1846); some moons are missing.

11 Pocket Globes. English. Left to right: planetarium by Newton, *c.* 1850; globes by Newton, after 1817; by Newton, dated 1818; by Dudley Adams, *c.* 1810; celestial globe by Newton, *c.* 1850.

12 Sea Astrolabe. Probably Portuguese, dated 1555; brass, weighs 6 lb 6 oz (2·9 kg).

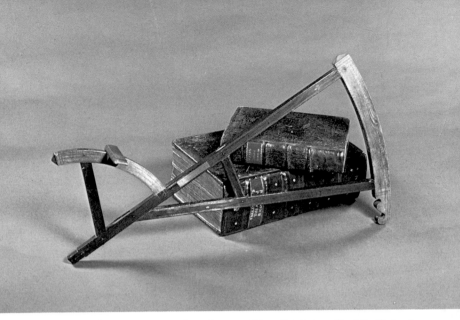

13 Back-staff. English, *c.* 1746. Owner's name: Thos. Dutch Jany 20, 1746. Made of lignum vitae and boxwood; two vanes missing.

14 Artificial Horizon. English, late 19th-century. The mahogany tray holds the mirror of liquid mercury, protected by the angled glass cover.

15 Octant. English, early 19th-century, signed *W. & T. Gilbert, London*.

16 Sextant. Dutch, 1790, signed *G. Hulst van Keulen Fecit Amsterdam* No 276.

17 Azimuth Compass. English, *c.* 1790, signed *McCULLOCH PATENT*.

18 Dip Circle. English, *c.* 1850, signed *L. Cassella, Maker to the Admiralty & Ordinance, London, No. 58*.

19 Binnacle. English, *c*. 1874. Compass card signed *J. J. WILSON & SON SUNDER-LAND*. From the brigantine *The Lady of Avenel*, Falmouth.

20 Traverse Board. Probably Dutch, 19th-century. Wood painted green.

21 Marine Chronometer. English, *c.* 1840, signed *John R. Arnold London Invt. et Fecit*; numbered 305. Label of retailer in lid, Peter Walther, Baltimore, USA.

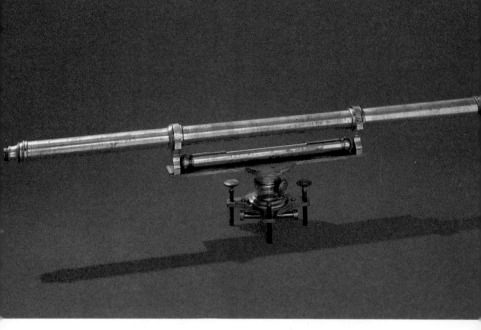

22 Surveyor's Level. English, mid 18th-century, signed *Jos Jackson LONDON*.

23 Theodolite. English, *c.* 1830, signed *W & S Jones Holborn London*.

24 Circumferentor. English, mid 18th-century, signed *Streatfield, London*.

25 Plane Table with Alidade. English, *c.* 1700. Compass card signed *Iohn Worgan Londini fecit 1696*.

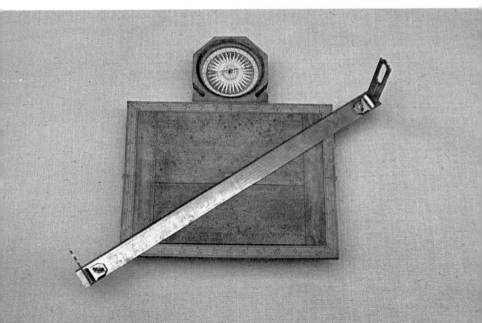

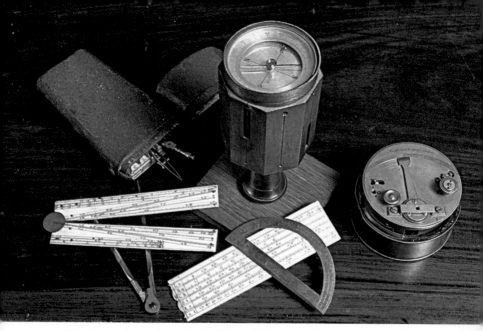

26 Left: Drawing Instruments, English, *c.* 1800, sector, dividers, plotting scale, protractor. Centre: Surveyor's Cross, French, *c.* 1900. Right: Pocket Sextant, *c.* 1840, signed *Smith, London.*

27 Surveyor's Wheel (Waywiser). English, *c.* 1830, signed *Dollond London.* Wheel diameter 32 in (82 cm) giving circumference of 100 in (250 cm).

28 Left: Pocket Compass. English, mid 19th-century. Right: Prismatic Compass. English, *c.* 1825, signed *SCHMALCALDER'S PATENT, 399 STRAND, LONDON.*

29 Drawing Instruments. English, 18th-, 19th-century. Folding 3 ft rule; parallel rulers; rectangular protractor; three sectors; plotting scale; Coggeshall rule.

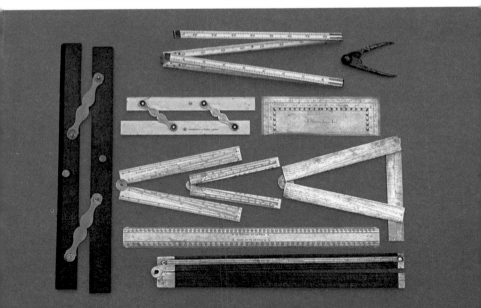

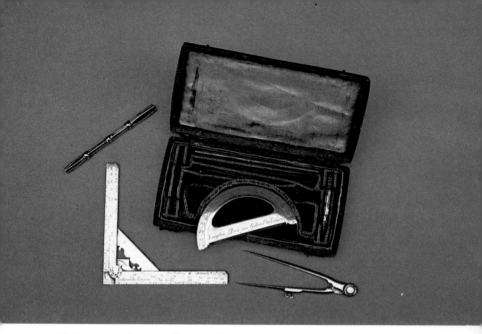

30 Drawing Instruments. French, mid 18th-century, signed *Langlois AParis aux Galleries du Louvre*; sector, protractor, dividers, pen-holder, all in silver.

31 Left: Ellipsograph. English, *c.* 1815, signed *W & S JONES 30 Holborn London*; John Farey's design. Right: Elliptical Trammel, English, late 18th-century.

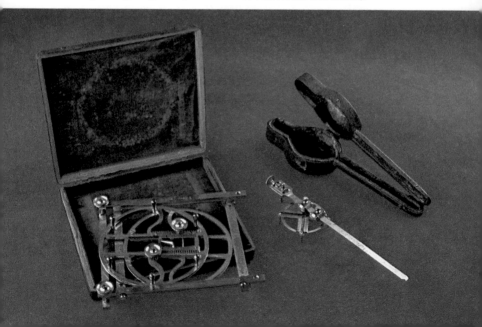

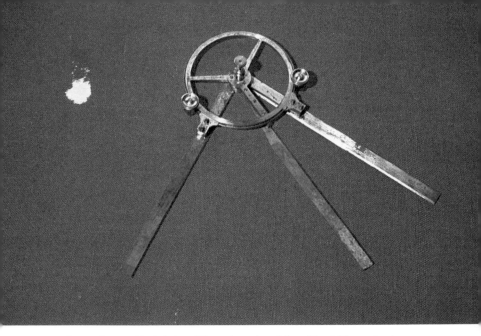

32 Station Pointer. English, late 19th-century, signed *Troughton & Simms, London.*

33 Abaci. Top: Chinese, *c.* 1900. Left: Russian, *c.* 1950. Right: Japanese, *c.* 1970.

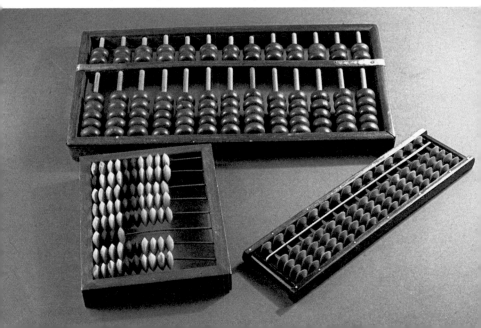

34 Napier's Bones. English, late 17th-century.

35 Slide Rules. English. Left to right: Ewart's Cattle Gauge, late 19th-century; Coggeshall Rule, early 19th-century; Everard Gauger's Slide Rule, late 18th-century; Gauging Rod for casks, early 19th-century.

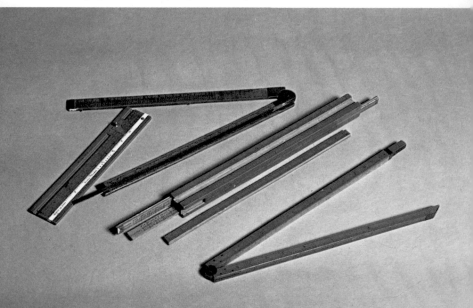

36 Compound Microscope. English, *c.* 1725. Early Culpeper type, made of lignum vitae, gold-tooled leather, brass, with oak case.

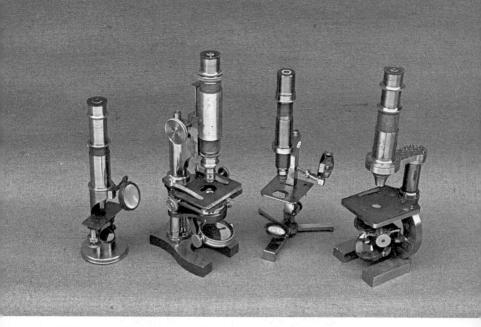

37 Compound Microscopes. Left to right: Drum type, French, *c.* 1850, by Chevallier; French, *c.* 1900, by Nachet; Italian, *c.* 1840, by Amici; German, *c.* 1860, by Zeiss.

38 Compound Microscope. English, dated 1845, signed *Powell & Lealand Makers, London*. Accessories shown are stage, fish-plate, tweezers, condenser, objective can.

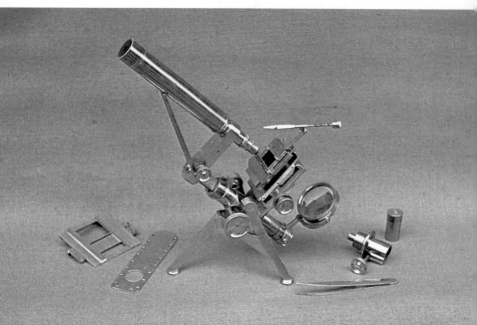

39 Telescopes. English. Left to right, top: Opera Glasses, *c.* 1840, *c.* 1750; Binoculars, *c.* 1890; Opera Glass, *c.* 1780. Middle: Reflector, *c.* 1750; Refractors, *c.* 1790, *c.* 1780. Bottom: *c.* 1830.

40 Left to right: Camera Obscura. English, early 19th-century; Camera Lucida, English, signed *Dollond London*; Scioptic Ball, English, late 18th-century.

41 Telescope, Gregorian Reflector. English, *c.* 1752, signed *JAMES SHORT LONDON 109/767=12*. The focal length of objective mirror is 12 in (30 cm), and aperture is 3 in (7·5 cm).

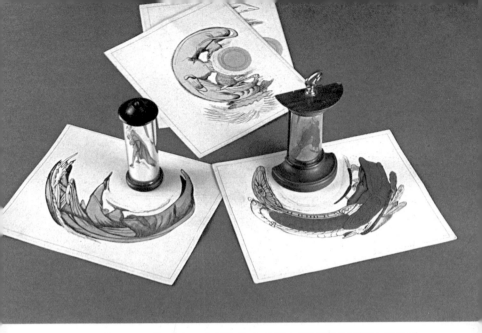

42 Anamorphoscopes. English, early 19th-century. The distorted drawings are recti-
fied when seen in the cylindrical mirrors.

43 Praxinoscope Theatre. French, *c.* 1890. The paper strip is viewed in a series of
rotating mirrors via a glass plate which can reflect a picture as a background for
the moving figure.

44 Stereo-viewer. English, *c.* 1865. Photographic pairs are slotted in at the wide end, and are viewed through two lenses to give the illusion of solidity.

45 Model of a Piledriver. Dutch, *c.* 1756, by Jacob Kley, Rotterdam, made in mahogany and brass. Shows how bridge piles are driven into a river bed. Invented *c.* 1738 for the building of Westminster Bridge, London.

46 Model of Pisa's Leaning Tower. Possibly Dutch, late 18th-century. Elaborate alabaster model to illustrate theory of stability, when centre of gravity is perpendicularly above the base.

47 Lodestone. Russian, *c.* 1790. Inscribed in Russian on the case: 'The stone weighs 12 funt. Lifts 1 pud, 20 funt (i.e. 4·8 kg and 24 kg)'.

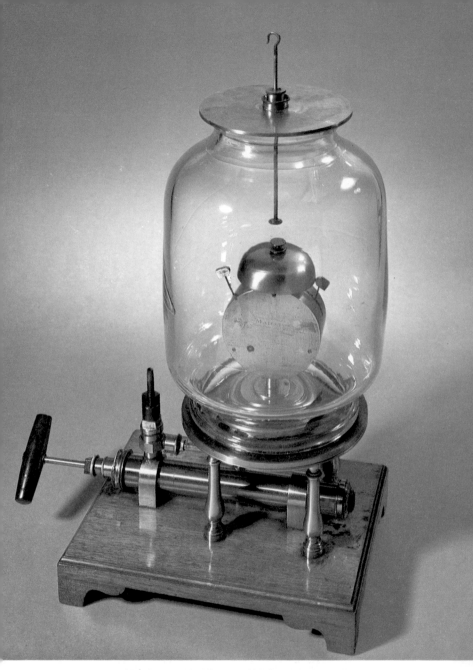

48 Air Pump. English, *c.* 1830, by Watkins & Hill. Single horizontal barrel, on a mahogany base clamped to a table. Clockwork bell cannot be heard when in a vacuum.

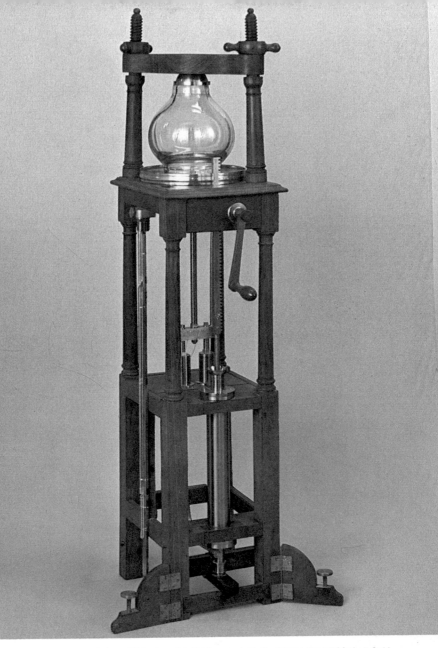

49 Air Pump. English, *c.* 1785, signed *I. B. Haas Invt, By the King's Patent Made & Sold by J. H. Hurter, London.* A fine example of a double-barrelled pump. The mechanism was patented by Jacob Haas in 1783; Hurter was his business partner.

50 Model of Archimedean Screw. English, late 18th-century. A tube in helical form will raise water when turned. Here an ivory ball climbs to the top of a cut-away tube.

51 Hydrometers. English. Left: six glass floats for densities greater than water, c. 1820, by Twaddell, Glasgow. Right: brass, of Clarke's design for Excise use, c. 1810, by Dring & Fage, London.

52 Electrical Machine. English, *c.* 1820, signed *DOLLOND LONDON*. A glass disc frictional electrical generator, bought by the Utrecht Physical Society in about 1820. On the right is a Leyden Jar, decorated with a chinoiserie pattern.

53 Thunder House. Dutch, *c.* 1790, signed *Ino. Cuthbertson Amsterdam.* The roof, walls, back and front are hinged together. When the lightning conductors are earthed, all is well; when not earthed, the house collapses when a spark is delivered.

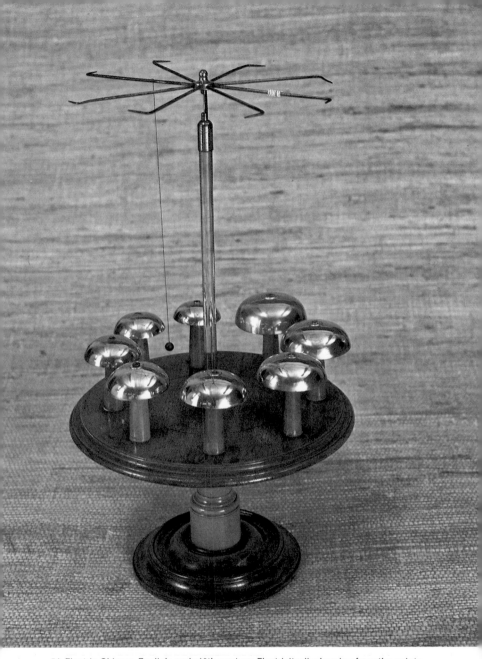

54 Electric Chimes. English, early 19th-century. Electricity discharging from the points of the metal spinner cause it to rotate, and a small clapper suspended from it strikes each bell in turn.

55 Volta's Hydrogen Lamp. Italian, c. 1792. The globe holds hydrogen, and the top reservoir water, which forces the gas to the jet orifice. The gas is lit by an electric spark. Invented in 1779 by Alessandro Volta.

56 Thermometer. English, *c.* 1830, signed *J. NEWMAN, 122 REGENT STRT LONDON.*
Registers maximum and minimum, the 1782 design of James Six.

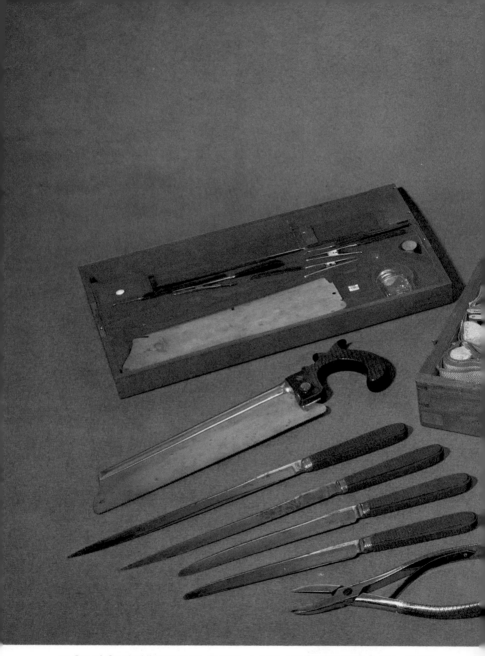

57 Set of Surgical Instruments. English, *c.* 1853, signed *SAVIGNY & CO., 67 ST JAMES'S ST. LONDON.* Taken by U. W. Evans, M.D., to the Crimea. Florence Nightingale directed him into hospital administration, so the set was never used.

58 Barometer. English, *c.* 1800, signed *Dom. Sala, LONDON.* Spirit thermometer on the left, and on the right is Amonton's double barometer design of 1688, which has oil between the mercury columns.

59 Baromètre liègeois. Left: English, late 19th-century, signed *F. DAVIDSON & Co. 29 GRT PORTLAND ST.* Right: Belgian, 19th-century. Water level rises in spout for storm (low pressure), lowers for fine weather.

60 Spectroscope. English, *c.* 1875, signed *John Browning, London.*

61 Steelyard and Bow-spring Scale. English, late 19th-century.

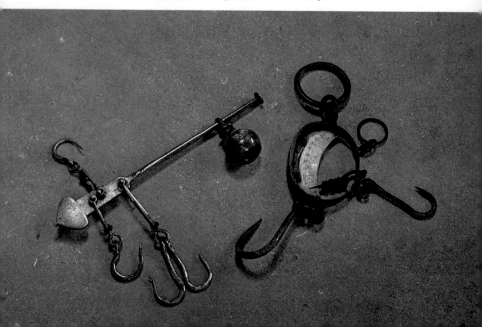

62 Coin Balances. English (except one). Left to right, top: *c.* 1790; *c.* 1775 (suspended); *c.* 1750 with carat weights, by Timo Robert. Bottom: *c.* 1775; *c.* 1780, by T. Harrison; German, *c.* 1700.

63 Apothecaries' Balances. English, late 19th-century. Bottom: Chinese Opium Scales, 19th-century.

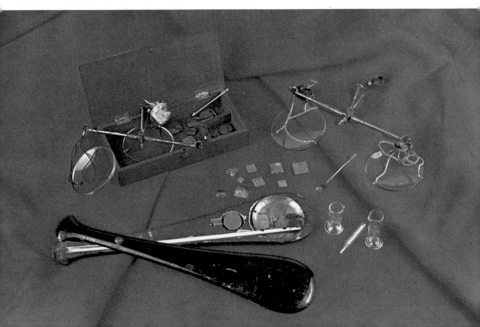

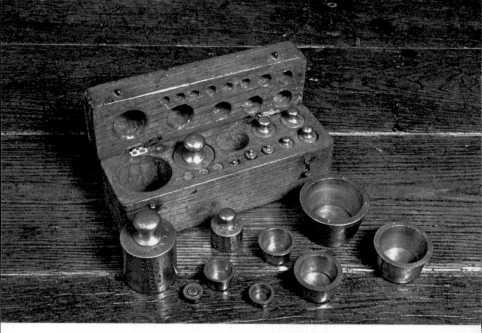

64 Sets of Weights. In elm case, Dutch, 1820; weights from 1 gm to 1 kg (=1 Ned. Pond). Right: Cupweights. English, *c.* 1905; Troy weights, $\frac{1}{4}$ to 16 oz.

65 Left: Dutch measure, 1858; English $\frac{1}{2}$ lb weight, *c.* 1860. Right: English Winchester Quart, 1817. Centre: English Standard Yard, 1837; English Yardstick, 1750; German Ell, 1786. Bottom: Russian Bismar, 1724.

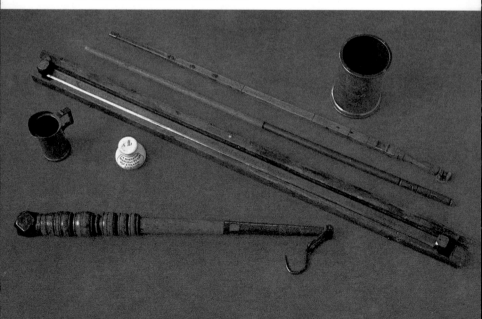

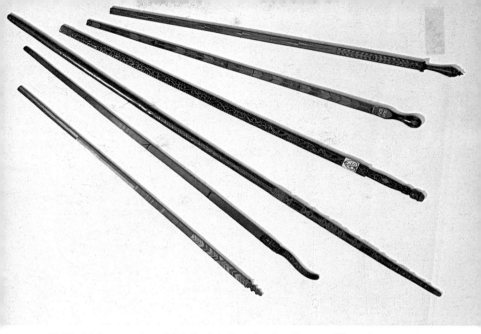

66 Ells (cloth measuring sticks). English, Scandinavian, German, 18th-century, except the longest, 1806.

67 Medical Equipment. English, 19th-century. Left to right, top: stethoscope; cupping set; cupping glasses; stethoscope; spirit lamp. Bottom: cauteriser, by Weiss; pair of scarificators, by Smith.

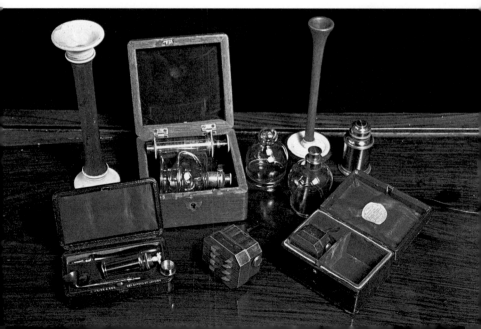

68 Medicine Chest. English, *c.* 1800, signed *DALMAHOY, LONDON*. Mahogany chest, with drawers, bottles, and boxes of medicines.

69 Demonstration Ophthalmoscope. Possibly German, late 19th-century. Twelve examples of the *fundus oculi* to be inserted in the brass model eye.

common in the seventeenth century, have diamond-shaped beads, which are disposed with 1 in the upper section and 4 in the lower. Russian and Polish abacuses have wooden beads on wire rods, with 10 on each wire, the two middle ones, 5 and 6, painted black. As well as examples of Far Eastern and Eastern European abacuses from the nineteenth and twentieth centuries, it is possible to find examples of bead frames made for teaching children in Britain during the Victorian and Edwardian periods.

It is interesting to note that modern mathematics and modern technology have brought back the principle of the abacus, after a period of pen reckoning.

Napier's Bones

The techniques of adding and subtracting were well established from antiquity, but by the sixteenth century it became necessary for navigation and surveying to develop the new technique of multiplication. This was not possible with Roman numerals, but the introduction of Arabic mathematics made it feasible although very tedious. John Napier, laird of Merchiston in Scotland, devised logarithmic tables, and published his discovery in 1614. He wrote that the multiplication and division of great numbers is troublesome, involving tedious expenditure of time, and subject to 'slippery errors'. His tables reduced these difficulties to simple addition and subtraction, and won immediate recognition. In 1617, he published another book which included the technique of using the rectangular rods inscribed with numbers which became known as Napier's bones. Each rod is engraved with a table of multiples of a particular digit, the 10s and units separated by an oblique line. To obtain a product of 123 × 4, the rods 1, 2 and 3 are put alongside each other, and the result is read off by adding the numbers in the fourth row: |0/4|0/8|1/2|. The adding is done along the diagonal. The number of rods in a set is basically 10, plus extras representing squares and cubes. The rods are usually made of boxwood or ivory, and are often contained in a box or case. Examples can still be found, as the bones were in use until the end of the eighteenth century. Napier's bones are sometimes found associated with an abacus.

Slide Rule

Another calculating instrument, elegant in its simplicity, is the slide rule. It is based on logarithms, and its origin is in the scale devised by Edmund Gunter in about 1607, and published by him in 1623. The

Gunter scale is composed of two scales of the logarithms from 1 to 10 placed end to end, and used with a pair of dividers to connect proportions between numbers on the two scales, so allowing multiplication and division to be performed. By 1621, William Oughtred had invented the slide rule, by putting two Gunter scales side by side. There was a controversy between Oughtred and his pupil, Richard Delamain, over the invention of the circular slide rule, which Delamain published under the name of the Mathematical Ring in 1630, and Oughtred published as Circles of Proportion in 1632. The third form of slide rule was also produced in the 1620s, the helical slide rule, with the lines drawn on the surface of a cylinder, invented by Thomas Browne, a joiner.

The two most commonly found types of slide rule in the eighteenth and nineteenth centuries were the Coggeshall and the Everard. That typically used by carpenters is named after Henry Coggeshall, a mathematician who invented it in 1677. It is a two-foot jointed rule, made of boxwood with a brass hinge and end-caps, with a brass slider in one arm. The slider bears a Gunter-type logarithm scale; on one side of it is a conventional double 1–10 scale, while on the other side is a broken Gunter scale from 4 to 40, which is called the girt line, for measuring the volume of timber. On the back is the 24-inch rule, and on the back of the brass slider is a 12-inch rule, so that the whole thing can measure a yard. Also marked on the rule is a table which gives the price in pounds, shillings and pence of various units of timber. Along the edge of the rule is a scale dividing the foot into 100 parts, a foretaste of metrication.

The Excise officer's gauge for assessing the duty on wines, spirits and ale was nearly square in section, with sliders in all four sides. This was the Everard slide rule, invented by Thomas Everard, a gauger in the Excise at Southampton in the 1680s. It is a foot long, and an inch square, with inset Gunter's scales, and is marked with standard points important for Excise use, that include WG—wine gallon; AG—ale gallon; MB—malt bushel.

A very large cylindrical slide rule was patented in 1881 by Edwin Thacher, and made in New York; but the handiest cylindrical rule, equivalent to 8 times the length of a normal slide rule, and giving the possibility of reading to 3 or 4 places of decimals, was the invention of Professor G. Fuller at the turn of the century. This was in general use in the early twentieth century, and examples are found in sale rooms. The Fuller slide rule was sold in a box, and was fixed by its handle to a bracket at one end of the box when in use.

The traditional, rectangular slide rule is made of boxwood, with brass fittings. Circular rules were made of brass, while cylindrical ones were sometimes printed on paper from engraved plates, and mounted on wood. The invention of ivorine in the 1890s, a trade name for a white synthetic material, gave added scope for the development of more accurate engraved scales for all three types of slide rule.

Calculating Machines

Arithmetical machines, using gearing to speed up calculation, began to be devised at the beginning of the seventeenth century. There were five main types of machine.

Addition machine. The first was devised by Blaise Pascal, a Frenchman, who, after many attempts, produced his definitive model in 1645, and had it manufactured for sale. Samuel Morland, Master of Mechanicks to King Charles II in 1681, produced his version of an adding machine in the 1660s.

Addition machine to be used for multiplication. This was made by Gottfried Leibnitz in 1672.

Multiplication machine. This was invented by Léon Bollés in 1888.

Difference machine. Two separate models were invented, devised by Johan Helfrich von Muller in 1786, and by Charles Babbage in 1822.

Analytical machine. A prototype was invented by Babbage in 1834.

Of these machines, the first three types were actually produced commercially, and examples are to be found, dating from the early nineteenth century. In about 1820, C. X. Thomas, who had a workshop in Paris, produced what he called his 'arithmometer', which consisted of a long wooden box, with numbers appearing in brass-framed 'windows', and a handle. His machines bear his name. An imitation, which was circular in shape, was patented by Joseph Edmondson of Halifax in Yorkshire. A later patent was taken out by S. Tate in 1903, in the rectangular form. One example in a British museum was used in 1910 by the Royal Automobile Club for speed trials. The perfection of the arithmetical machine was made by Curta of Liechtenstein, and consisted of a little cylinder which can be held in one hand, with a handle at the top. This type of machine was used by scientists and engineers in the 1950s, and was superseded only by the electronic calculator.

5
Optical Instruments

The Greeks understood the properties of mirrors and burning glasses and they studied geometrical optics, but the first person to make a study of lenses was the Islamic philosopher, Alhazan, at the beginning of the eleventh century. His work influenced Roger Bacon, a Franciscan who made a great reputation as a university teacher at Oxford just over two hundred years later. Bacon has been credited with the invention of spectacles, but it is more likely that he foresaw rather than invented them. Eye-glasses were almost certainly first produced in Pisa in the late thirteenth century, and were in general use throughout Europe during the Middle Ages. Yet no one seems to have had the idea of placing one lens in front of another to make a telescope or microscope, the difference between the two instruments, in these early days, being dependent upon the distance separating the two lenses.

Though Galileo is popularly supposed to have invented the telescope, and was certainly one of its early users, the inventors of both the compound microscope and the refracting telescope (as opposed to the reflecting telescope which used not lenses, but mirrors of polished metal) were Hans and Zacharias Janssen, spectacle makers of Middleburg in the Netherlands, at a date between 1590 and 1610. The early compound microscopes were certainly not of much use by today's standards, though what they revealed appeared marvellous at the time. The glass was poor in quality, and chromatic and spherical aberrations blurred the image. The history of the development of the microscope is the history of the banishment of these defects from the image.

Chromatic aberration is caused by the unequal refraction of light rays of different colour, which means that the blue and red ends of the spectrum come to a focus at different points, resulting in a coloured edge to the microscopic image. With a spherical lens (non-spherical lenses have only been produced in very recent times), the focal point of those rays that pass through near the edge of the lens come to a focus closer to the lens than do the central rays. As rays from all parts of the object pass through all parts of the lens, the whole of the image is unsharp.

It was because of these deficiencies that one of the most successful and remarkable of the early microscopists, a Dutch draper called Antoni van Leeuwenhoek, used not a compound but a simple microscope, consisting of a tiny bead lens, held up to the eye in a metal plate. With infinite patience and skill, Van Leeuwenhoek achieved significantly higher resolution than was possible with a typical compound microscope even in 1800, a century or more later than he was working.

Nevertheless, the compound microscope had already made sufficiently striking observations possible. In 1660, Marcello Malpighi observed the blood capillaries, thus providing the crucial evidence to confirm William Harvey's theory of the circulation of the blood. Following Malpighi's observations, nearly every microscope sold for the next 200 years had as an accessory the fish- or frog-plate, to hold a specimen so that the circulation of the blood could be observed. The other subjects popular with seventeenth-century microscopists are all described and illustrated in Robert Hooke's *Micrographia*, published in 1665 by the man who was Curator of Experiments to the newly-founded Royal Society of London, and a former assistant to Robert Boyle.

During the early years of the eighteenth century, considerable advances were made in the design of the microscope stand, using brass, rather than the earlier pasteboard and wood, and giving the instrument greater stability and finer adjustment. But the first really important optical improvement was the work of John Dollond, the son of a Huguenot weaver, whose hobby was geometry. In middle life, he joined his son, Peter, in his instrument-making business, and achieved the remarkable feat of correcting chromatic aberration in the telescope, by using a combination of crown glass and flint glass for the lenses. The Dollonds marketed lens combinations of this type from 1758, for use in telescopes. The much smaller lenses needed to produce the same correction for the compound microscope presented greater technical problems, and were not produced until the end of the century, by an Amsterdam instrument maker, Harmanus van Deijl.

During the 1820s, the problem of making objectives for the microscope that were not only achromatic but also free from spherical aberration was tackled in a variety of ways, including the further development of the reflecting microscope, and the use of lenses made of gem stones. In 1830, however, came the publication, in the *Philosophical Transaction of the Royal Society*, of a paper by Joseph Jackson Lister, in which he described his method of using two achromatic lens combinations at a certain distance apart to eliminate spherical aberra-

113

tion from the image. Lister, a wine merchant, and the father of the great medical pioneer, Lord Lister, crossed the final technical frontier in the development of the optical microscope, which became, during the Victorian period, a vital tool in medical and other scientific research.

Until John Dollond's work on achromatic lens combinations for the refracting telescope bore fruit in the latter half of the eighteenth century, the best astronomical telescopes were of the reflecting type. The first reflecting telescope was made in 1668, to his own design and with his own hands, by Isaac Newton. In the eighteenth century, the London instrument-making trade included many fine telescope makers, of whom the most notable was the Scotsman, James Short. His skill at founding and polishing by hand the pairs of metal mirrors which provided the optics of his telescopes was such that they were bought by most of the observatories in Europe and the New World. Short's achievement was built upon and extended by William Herschel at the end of the eighteenth century. Large reflecting telescopes were in use in observatories throughout the nineteenth century, and, with ever bigger mirrors, are still employed today.

The early refracting telescopes suffered from the poor quality of glass used for their lenses, and from aberrations in the image. The extremely long tube required to achieve a focus made them unwieldy and unpractical. But from the mid-eighteenth century onward, refracting telescopes were used for nautical and military purposes, and, as the optics improved, for astronomical work as well.

Microscopes

The two basic types of microscope are simple and compound. The simple microscope consists of one lens; or, in some cases, of one lens composed of two or three elements, which simply looks like a single, rather thick lens. The compound microscope has at least two, usually three or more lenses, which have to be held at a fair distance from each other by being mounted in a rigid tube, made of pasteboard, ivory, or, most commonly, brass. The typical eighteenth-century compound microscope has a small objective lens (there are probably five or six alternatives to choose from in the accompanying kit of accessories), a field lens from one to three inches (2.5 to 7.5 cm) in diameter, placed in the middle of the tube, and an eye lens (closest to the eye), which is bigger than the objective lens, but smaller than the field lens. The sizes and positions of the lenses vary; Benjamin Martin, for example, often had five lenses in his microscopes. In the eighteenth century nearly all these lenses would have been double convex. In the nineteenth century, when serious design was for the first time applied to the optical system of the microscope, lens elements became much more complex. The multiple objectives of Victorian microscopes should not be dismounted for examination, except by an expert.

Seventeenth-century Microscopes Few microscopes from this period remain, even in museums. They were made from wood, pasteboard, and vellum, which was often decorated with gold tooling. Leading makers were John Marshall and John Yarwell. Of recent years, there have sometimes appeared in the salerooms microscopes with a seventeenth-century optical tube mounted on a stand of a much later period.

The simple microscope invented and used by Antoni van Leeuwenhoek in the late seventeenth century consisted of a tiny bead lens set in a metal plate, with a pin mount to hold the specimen. There are fewer than ten genuine Leeuwenhoek microscopes known to exist, and all are in collections. It should be noted that a considerable number of imitations were produced, and these are sometimes found on sale.

Screw-barrel Microscope In the early part of the eighteenth century, many simple microscopes of this type were produced, made of ivory or brass, and generally contained in a black fishskin or leather box. The optical tube may have a side handle that screws in place, or may mount on a brass pillar with a tripod foot. Most of these microscopes will be unsigned, but some may bear the name E. (Edmund) Culpeper.

Culpeper-type Microscope This type of compound microscope was first produced in the 1720s. The optical tube, made of wood, pasteboard, and leather fits into a cylindrical support covered in rayskin (often called shagreen). This is held by three legs, rising from a circular wooden base, with a simple brass stage between the legs. These microscopes were originally supplied with a wooden case of pyramidal shape, made from oak, or, later, mahogany. Those retailed by Culpeper himself have his trade card stuck at the back of the case, showing his sign of the crossed daggers. Later models in the same form have a wooden box foot with a drawer to hold accessories. This pattern continued until the mid-nineteenth century, but leather, pasteboard, and rayskin were gradually superseded by brass, until, by 1780, the whole instrument, with the exception of the box foot, was made of brass. Many examples of the later form of the Culpeper-type microscope exist, but the majority are unsigned. However, names that may be found are Adams, Nairne, Nairne & Blunt, and W & S Jones. This form of microscope was imitated on the continent, and some Dutch and French unsigned examples are to be found.

Cuff-type Microscope Another common and important type of compound microscope was that first made by John Cuff, to the design of Henry Baker in 1743. The instrument is similar to Marshall's design from the seventeenth century, in that the body tube was supported on a bracket fixed to a side pillar. This pillar is fitted with a well-made focusing arrangement, which allows for the first time some exactitude in adjusting the microscope for use. The instrument is mounted on a mahogany box foot and was originally contained in a mahogany pyramidal case.

Cuff-type microscopes may bear the signatures of Dollond, Gilbert, and Martin. In Paris, Claude Passemant adopted Cuff's design for the compound microscope, and his workshop had a considerable production in the mid-eighteenth century.

Benjamin Martin's Designs By the 1780s, the range of microscopes on the market included, as well as the Culpeper-type and the Cuff-type, a third model, designed by Benjamin Martin. This had a tripod foot which folded flat, and a compass joint at the base of the pillar which enabled the pillar to be moved to an angle away from the vertical, to make use easier. This design was sold by Martin himself and by Adams and W & S Jones. Variations on this model were developed and modified into the nineteenth century.

Another design of microscope which continued into this century was Benjamin Martin's drum. This consisted of a cylindrical tube with a portion cut away near the base to allow light to fall on the substage mirror. It was rather like a very compact Culpeper-type microscope. This model was cheap to buy and therefore very popular with amateur microscopists in the period 1820 to 1850. There are a good many examples in brass still on the market, generally unsigned. It continued to be available as a cheap toy well into the twentieth century.

Naturalists' Microscopes In the latter half of the eighteenth century, the study of botany became extremely popular, and several portable versions of the microscope were designed for naturalists. One of the first of these to achieve wide sales was the Withering botanic micro-

116

scope, invented in 1792 by the famous botanist, Dr William Withering. The pillar, holding a simple lens and a wooden stage, is fixed to the inside of the hinged lid of a small box. When the box is opened, the microscope automatically positions itself for use.

Another version, often known as the Cary-type, because so many were retailed by W. Cary, also packed away into a pocket-sized mahogany box. Invented by Gould *c.* 1820, this microscope consisted of an optical tube with a conical nose-piece, mounted on a slim pillar with rack focusing on the stage.

Nuremberg Microscopes The town of Nuremberg in Bavaria has long been famous for its superb craftsmen, and also became known as a centre for the manufacture and distribution of simple wooden toys, some of which were made in the Black Forest and the Austrian Tirol. Among these were microscopes made from soft wood, with draw-tubes of card and patterned paper, very light in weight and inexpensive. Two designs were popular, the Culpeper-type on three legs, and the drum-type, but rectangular rather than round in section. The majority of these microscopes were the work of two traders, whose initials are burnt into the base of the instrument with a hot iron: 'I.M.' and 'J.F.F.'. Contrary to what has often been written, the majority of these instruments date from the first half of the nineteenth century, though a few may have been made at the end of the eighteenth.

Mid-Victorian Compound Microscope Following the production of achromatic objective lenses, and the work of J. J. Lister in overcoming spherical aberration, the optical microscope moved steadily towards the achievement of the highest resolution of which it was capable. It became an important scientific instrument, as makers such as Andrew Ross, James Smith, and Hugh Powell improved the rigidity of the optical tube, and the coarse and fine focusing. The firms who were world-famous for top quality instruments were Ross, Powell & Lealand, and Smith & Beck. But there were a great many other makers providing for the amateur market, and many microscopes of this period carry the names of optical firms which merely retailed instruments. From 1860, binocular tubes were provided for many microscopes, to make extended use easier and less tiring, so Victorian microscopes of this type are to be found. Microscopes were also sold in large mahogany chests, beautifully fitted with up to 100 accessories, many of which would never have been used. On the continent, the German optical instrument trade rose to prominence with the new designs of Utschneider and Fraunhofer around 1810, and later with those of Carl Zeiss of Jena, and Ernst Leitz of Wetzlar. In France, leading makers were the Chevalier family, and the firm of Nachet. With the greatly increased production of the late nineteenth and early twentieth centuries, new models were produced every few years by leading firms, and catalogues of the firms are the best source of information on dating and identifying their microscopes. Some old catalogues, for example those of Nachet, have been reprinted recently.

An advertisement in a book published in 1865 lists the following British and foreign microscope makers. British: Baker, London; Bryson, Edinburgh; Charles Collins, London; H & W Crouch, London; Dancer, Manchester; Field, Birmingham; S. Highley, London; King, Bristol; W. Ladd, London; Murray & Heath, London; Parkes & Son, Birmingham; Pillischer, London; Powell & Lealand, London; Ross, London; Salmon, London; Smith, Beck & Beck, London. Foreign: Amici, Modena: Benèche, Berlin; Brunner, Paris; Chevalier, Paris; Hartnack & Oberhauser, Paris; Hasert, Eisenach; Kellner, Wetzlar; G. & S. Merz, Munich; A. Mirand, Paris; Nachet, Paris; Ploesl, Vienna; Schröder, Hamburg; F. W. Schiek, Berlin; Zeiss, Jena.

Telescopes
Refractors In a refracting telescope, all the optical parts are lenses, and the name derives from the fact that light is refracted when it enters glass. This is the earliest type of telescope, and developed in three different forms. The first is the astronomical telescope which has two lenses, both of which converge the light, and are known as positive lenses, producing the image upside down (which presents no problems for observations of the heavens). This type of refractor is very seldom found today. The second form of refracting telescope is that for terrestrial use, having a three-lens erecting eyepiece system in addition to the objective lens. All these lenses are positive, and the resulting image is upright. Examples can still be found of this type of telescope from the late seventeenth and early eighteenth centuries, made from pasteboard covered with dyed vellum or fish-skin. In the mid-eighteenth century, this type of telescope had long wooden tubes with brass lens mounts. From 1800, improved techniques of making brass tubing made telescopes far more compact, with shorter sections of tube that nested or 'telescoped' into each other. The brass body tube was often painted, or sometimes covered with wood or leather, and, in the case of naval

telescopes, plaited rope. Some were laquered and elaborately decorated. The third type of refractor consists of an objective which is a converging positive lens, with a diverging, or negative, eye lens. These telescopes are known as the Galilean type, because Galileo popularised this arrangement from 1610. The advantage is cheapness, because only two lenses need to be figured, and the image is upright. The disadvantage is that magnification is not great. This arrangement was, in the eighteenth and nineteenth centuries, chiefly restricted to opera and field glasses. Opera glasses of the late eighteenth century and the Regency period are often remarkably opulent, made of ivory or ebony, encrusted with pearls or ormolu decoration. In the late Victorian period, many binocular field glasses were produced to the Galilean pattern, as are present day opera glasses.

Reflectors The common reflecting telescope produces an erect image, and was the eighteenth century's most popular telescope, because it did not suffer from chromatic aberration. Also, it was considerably shorter in length than the terrestrial refracting telescope, and could be made with a larger aperture, to gather more light. Again, there are three types of reflecting telescope. The Gregorian reflector, named after James Gregory, the Scottish mathematician, has a concave objective mirror, and a concave secondary mirror, which reflects the light from the objective through a small hole in the middle of the objective mirror into the eyepiece. A similar-looking reflector is known as the Cassegrainian type, where the secondary mirror is convex and the image is inverted. Not many of these were made, but they are occasionally found today. With both these forms, the telescope is put to the eye and pointed straight at the object to be viewed.

With the other type, the Newtonian reflector, the observer stands at right angles to the line of view. This is because the objective mirror collects light and reflects it on to a small, plain mirror set at $45°$ to the axis of the telescope. The eyepiece is, therefore, at right angles to the tube, and at the top end of the telescope. The most popular form of the Newtonian telescope was that produced at the end of the eighteenth century by William Herschel for astronomical observations. The smallest Herschel telescope has a metal mirror of $6\frac{1}{4}$ inches ($15\frac{1}{2}$ cm) diameter, and is of 7 foot (2.1 m) focal length. The instrument is held in a large mahogany frame. These instruments are occasionally to be found in salerooms today, and fetch a price lower than one would expect because of their size.

Makers of refracting telescopes
From 1690 to 1710, the most popular makers of telescopes in Europe were John Yarwell and John Marshall of London. In the eighteenth century, the names of Dollond, Martin, and Ramsden appear most frequently on British-made instruments; in France, Passemant was the leading name, and in Holland, Harmanus van Deijl. During the early eighteenth century, three to four draw-tube telescopes of pasteboard covered with decorated paper, were made in Italy; the name of Leonardo Semitecolo appears on several. In the nineteenth century, a great many names of retailers of telescopes are found. Among the best-known firms of the mid-century are Tulley, Varley & Son, Salmon, Wray, Dixey, Watkins & Hill, Harris & Son, Dollond, Negretti & Zambra. One of the most prolific of French telescope-makers of the Napoleonic period was Lerebours, who supplied the navy, the Bureau des Longitudes, and many surveyors. Other leading French makers were Buron and Lebrun; among those in Germany were Kinzelbach of Württemberg and Busch of Prussia.

Makers of reflecting telescopes
The finest reflecting telescopes of the eighteenth century were made in London, where all the leading makers advertised as a matter of course in several languages. The reflectors of James Short found their way into most national observatories all over the world. Other leading names are those of Mann & Ayscough, Adams, Nairne and Dollond. In Holland, a leading maker was Jan van der Bildt of Franeker, who made Gregorian telescopes.

Optical Toys

Mirrors
Sight is the prime sense of man, and optics is the chief provider of illusions. Sight could therefore transmit effects that were thought to be magical. This is particularly evident with mirrors having curved surfaces. Arrangements of concave mirrors can give an illusion of an object being within reach. Anamorphoscopes make use of a rectifying mirror, either conical, cylindrical or pyramidal, to make normal a wildly distorted drawing, which can only be seen properly in the mirror. Concave and convex mirrors, mounted back to back, serve to illustrate the difference in the reflected images. Convex mirrors in dark glass were employed as a painting aid by Claude Lorrain, and are called after him.

Camera Obscura

The portable camera obscura consists of a rectangular box, made of oak in the early part of the eighteenth century, but later of mahogany, with a lens in one end, in an adjustable tube, and a mirror set at a 45° angle to reflect light onto a horizontal ground glass screen. There are 'straight-through' versions without the mirror. Another camera obscura accessory which can still be found is the scioptic ball, used for fitting into a window shutter. This is about the size of the wooden ball used in the game of bowls; inside the hollow ball, usually made of the very hard wood lignum vitae, are two lenses. The ball is set in a rectangular mount of mahogany. The ball mounting allows considerable movement to pick up a variety of scenes.

Camera Lucida

This invention of William Wollaston in 1806 used a prism to enable a scenic view and the artist's drawing paper to be seen simultaneously. It could be adapted for use with the microscope, to aid the drawing of microscopic objects.

Magic Lantern

The magic lantern, using light projected through a transparent slide and enlarged by a lens to produce an image on a screen, has existed since the mid-seventeenth century. Examples from the Victorian period can be found, but the majority of magic lanterns on sale will date from the early years of this century. The light source can be either an oil lamp, or gas, often provided by a portable gas cylinder; later, magic lanterns had a fitting for an electric bulb. Many slides for use with magic lanterns can be found, the most attractive being made of hand-painted glass.

Zograscope and Stereoscope

Optical illusions seem to have attracted elaborate Greek names. The zograscope of the mid-eighteenth century consisted of a lens and mirror for looking at coloured engravings, making them appear three-dimensional. It continued in use until at least 1870, but was joined in the 1830s by the stereoscope. Stereo-viewers could consist of boxes, or even large cabinets, often made of walnut, fitted with pairs of viewing lenses, and transparent glass slides. By 1900, stereo cards were being mass-produced, on which pairs of photographs were pasted. These were viewed through simple, hand-held, stereo-viewers, consisting of a pair of hooded lenses, and a clip to hold the photographic card. Some which survive have a hood of chased aluminium, and were made in the United States in the Edwardian period. The cards have views from all over the world, Rome, Chicago and the Holy Land being popular subjects.

Kaleidoscope
This consisted of a tube in which two mirrors at 60° to each other were used to make symmetrical patterns from a random collection of chippings of coloured glass. It was patented by David Brewster in 1817, and continues as a popular child's toy today.

Persistence of vision devices
The simple thaumatrope of 1825, a cardboard disc spun between the fingers with, for example, a drawing of a bird one side and its cage on the other, engaged the persistence of vision effect in the eye and marked the beginning of the road that led to the cinema. Other milestones on this road were the phenakistoscope of 1832 and the zoetrope of 1860. In these a series of drawings was viewed through slits in a rotating disc and a rotating drum respectively, so giving the impression of movement. The praxinoscope of 1877 was an elaboration of the zoetrope which made use of mirrors. It could be arranged with a frame to give the impression of a theatrical performance. Muybridge was the first to analyse the movement of animals when with a battery of forty cameras he photographed a horse galloping. The prints from these photographs were arranged on a wheel, called a zoogyroscope, which when spun in a projector recreated the movement. Toy versions of these wheels were made during the 1880s for projection in the magic lantern. After the turn of the century, when cine cameras had been produced, sets of prints were reproduced in small books whose pages were 'flipped' by the thumb, so giving an impression of movement. These flip books were cheap and had a considerable vogue.

Cameras
The origins of photography lie in two sciences, optics and chemistry. The optical forerunner of the camera, from which it gets its name, was the camera obscura, described above. The chemistry of photography began in the eighteenth century, when scientists were working on the photochemistry of silver salts. At the end of the century it was established that light at the violet end of the spectrum is specially effective in darkening silver chloride. The first fixed photographs, using bitu-

men of Judea as the sensitive substance, were made in France by Nicé-
phore Niepce between 1825 and 1827. Twelve years later, his colleague,
Louis Daguerre, published his invention of the first successful photographic process. Almost at the same time, an Englishman, William
Henry Fox Talbot, perfected his different process. So photographs
from the 1840s are almost without exception either the metal daguerro-
types, or the sepia, paper calotypes of the English process. In 1851,
Frederick Scott Archer invented the wet collodion process, and for the
next forty years wet plate photography was practised. The next big
change was slow to be adopted; although gelatin dry plates were invented in 1871, it was not until the late 1880s that they were sufficiently
perfected to bring in the new era of the hand-held camera and the snap-
shot.

The first Kodak camera, 1888, with the celluloid roll-film created for it.

The first photographic cameras were the direct descendants of the box camera obscura, which threw an image on a ground glass screen, and was used by amateur artists. Early cameras usually consisted of two boxes, one sliding within the other for focusing. To make them easier to transport, the boxes were often made to fold down. A camera of this type was used from 1856 by Lewis Carroll, author of *Alice in Wonderland*, who was a skilled photographer. In 'Hiawatha's Photographing' he describes the elaborate process of portrait photography, using a camera of 'sliding, folding rosewood'. By the end of the 1850s, the bellows camera was becoming popular, but it was still large, used either on a substantial stand in the studio, or on a tripod for field work. Early cameras were technically very simple, with no shutters because of the very long exposure time, and no separate viewfinder.

The introduction of relatively fast dry plates in the late 1870s meant that cameras made after 1880 are often hand-held, and have a shutter. They were equipped with magazines of plates or cut films, and had a changing mechanism to bring forward each plate or film for exposure. In 1888, roll film was introduced, and metal began to take the place of wood for camera construction. At the end of the nineteenth century, there was a vogue for so-called detective cameras, which were small hand cameras made to look like some common object, such as a watch, parcel, or handbag. These were the forerunners of the precision miniature camera. The first small, roll-film camera of the box type, was produced by Kodak in 1888, and, together with the folding bellows type, made photography into a popular amateur activity. The final landmarks in the development of photography were the arrival of the first miniature 35 mm camera in 1924, and the invention of polaroid hand cameras and film by Dr Edwin Land in the 1950s.

6
Philosophical Instruments

The seventeenth century was a time of rapid change, from the theories about the natural world based on Greek thought, to Newton and experimental philosophy. Experiment rather than argument had priority at the meetings of the Royal Society of London, which was founded in Christopher Wren's room at Gresham College in 1660. This led to the vogue for lectures illustrated by demonstrations of physical effects, both at universities, and as a form of popular entertainment. From the beginning of the eighteenth century, the popularity of the lecture demonstration spread across Europe from England and Holland, reaching from Poland to Portugal, and to Harvard College in New England. The lecturers made use of a large quantity of apparatus, and many from among their audiences would later buy similar pieces to entertain friends in their own homes. So the effect of the lecture demonstration was greatly to stimulate the manufacture of scientific apparatus.

This popular taste for experiment did not die out by the end of the eighteenth century, though it became somewhat modified. Much of the apparatus used in lectures came gradually to be employed for teaching elementary science in schools. The very same pieces of equipment that Benjamin Martin, travelling lecturer and later a leading instrument maker, took with him on his tours round the West country can be found illustrated in catalogues of suppliers of scientific equipment well into the twentieth century. Still a source of popular entertainment, other pieces of demonstration apparatus have reappeared as toys, for example, the 'drinking duck' based on the thermoscope of Galileo.

What the eighteenth century understood by philosophical instruments was apparatus used to demonstrate and study mechanics (including working models); magnetism; models of the heavens; hydrostatics and hydraulics; pneumatics; heat (including meteorology); optics and electricity. Chemistry was dealt with separately, and, for obvious reasons, was generally practised in the laboratory rather than at home. Old chemical equipment is rarely found today, because, being of glass or earthenware, it tended to get broken. Portable analytical kits are

From the catalogue of Chadburn Brothers, Sheffield, 1851.

to inspect the Exhibition Room of

BROTHERS,
PHILOSOPHICAL INSTRUMENT MAKERS
NURSERY STREET

PORTRAIT GALLERY

ALBERT.

...M. ET. VERITAS.

BAROMETERS.
Thermometers.

SYRINGES.
Galvanic Electrical
and
MAGNETIC APPARATUS.
Theodolites.

LEVELS &
Surveyors Instruments.
MODELS, &c.

ENGRVED BY BRADSHAW & BLACKLOCK, MANCHESTER.

FIELD.

Occupation, *mounted in Horn or Steel, from 1/ In Elastic Blue Steel, from 2/6 In Tortoise*
...Eye Preservers, Hand Spectacles & Eye Glasses in great variety. Articles Purchased of C. B⁵
...don and Continental Makers.
...ratis, *with Copperplate Engravings 1 Shilling each.*

{OPTICAL GLASS GRINDING ROOM.}
NURSERY STEAM WHEEL.
Admission by Ticket from C. B⁵

sometimes found, as are chemical balances, which are dealt with in Chapter 7. Optical instruments and astronomical models are described in Chapter 5 and 1, respectively. Of the vast range of apparatus used through more than two centuries to demonstrate natural phenomena, a selection of the items most commonly to be found by the collector is described here. The object is to help in identifying the apparatus, which is the most difficult part of collecting this class of objects. Many may have been made in this century, as schools are now turning out their old laboratory cupboards. But these are well worth preserving, and their design will almost certainly date back to the eighteenth century. The more elegant pieces, made of fine wood and polished brass, will date from earlier periods than the Victorian, and will command higher prices. The best source of identification for the entire range of philosophic apparatus is the catalogues produced from 1900 to the 1930s by firms of scientific apparatus manufacturers such as J J Griffin, and Baird & Tatlock.

Mechanics
Various mechanical effects may be found demonstrated by models.

Forces The various effects of different forces acting on moving bodies— for example, a boat crossing a flowing stream has to have its bows pointing upstream in order to travel straight across—were demonstrated by boards or frames with sets of pulleys and weights, known as parallelogram of forces boards.

Gravity Some of the most popular models are the Leaning Tower of Pisa, to show the line of the centre of gravity; a human figure of an acrobat, holding a balancing bar and poised on a pillar to show equilibrium; a double cone or cylinder so weighted that it will roll up a slope.

Inclined Plane Models to show the amount of force required to draw a carriage up slopes of different inclines.

Inertia The centrifugal machine, or 'whirling table', was used to demonstrate all the different effects of force acting on a mass in uniform circular motion. The same effect can be seen today in a spin-dryer, and has been used as a fairground sideshow, in which the centrifugal force of a revolving drum holds bodies against its walls. The gyroscope, still popular today as a toy, shows the same effect.

Levers and Pulleys Sets of levers and pulleys were made for demonstration. The pulley combinations were often mounted in a large wooden frame. Models of winches and jacks, both using the lever principle, were also made.

Fall, Projection and Momentum In the latter half of the eighteenth century, George Atwood, a mathematician, devised his fall machine, which was a 6-foot (1.8 m) high piece of apparatus, designed to show the laws of motion of bodies uniformly accelerated and retarded. It included a clock mechanism, measuring scale, and complicated arrangements of pulleys and weights. There were numerous accessories. Atwood fall machines do appear sometimes in salerooms. Also popular were boards on which a marble could be rolled to show the parabolic curve of a projectile. The effect of momentum and collision was demonstrated by a series of balls suspended side by side at the same height from a framework which can be swung to knock against each other. This has now become a modern toy.

Mechanical Models Models of hoists, cranes, mills and pile-drivers were popular, because they showed the practical application of mechanical principles. The use of a steam jet was known from Greek times, but steam harnessed to produce power was gradually developed through the seventeenth and eighteenth centuries, culminating with the work of James Watt in the 1760s. Models of the different types of steam engine bearing the names of the different inventors, for example Branca, Savery, Papin, Newcomen, were made for demonstration, and, later, miniature locomotives were also produced during the railway boom. Stationary steam engine models are within the price range of most collectors, but working models of steam locomotives are much more expensive.

Magnetism

A natural magnet, or lodestone, is a particular form of iron oxide, Fe_3O_4, found in various parts of the world but particularly in Siberia. There are very ancient references to the magnet in Chinese, Egyptian, Greek and Roman texts. The name 'magnet' comes from the Greek, for magnets were found in the Greek province of Magnesia. The Chinese for magnet translates as 'love-stone' and the French name is 'l'aimant'. The earliest practical application of the magnet was in the compass, whose origin in the West is traditionally assigned to Amalfi in Italy, in the twelfth century. Once the use of magnetised iron for direction finding was known, magnets became of commercial importance. Every seaman needed one to keep his compass needle magnetised. And magnets were also used as philosophical instruments, to demonstrate the power of magnetism. There was a demand for very large magnets from Siberia—the Ashmolean Museum in Oxford was presented with one in 1756 which would support 163 lbs (*c.* 74 kg). Russian lodestones are still occasionally to be found in filigree brass cases, on which are inscribed Russian letters and usually the weight that the magnet will support.

Pneumatics
Natural philosophers studied the nature and properties of air and gases, and were particularly concerned with creating a vacuum. Otto von Guerike of Magdeburg, in 1654, performed the classic vacuum experiment, by evacuating the air from two large iron hemispheres, fitted together. Once this had been done, no amount of force would tear the two halves apart. The so-called Magdeburg hemispheres were still being produced in the 1930s. Von Guerike used a very primitive air pump.

The first really practical single-cylinder air pump was devised by Robert Boyle and Robert Hooke, but it was Hauksbee who made the two-cylinder model that continued in general use in Britain, although on the Continent, large-bore, single-cylinders were usual. The air pump had a range of accessories. Air pumps may be found today, though the glass receiver is likely to be a replacement; the basic construction is of wood and brass.

Hydrostatics
Strictly speaking, this is the term used for the equilibrium of fluids, and the pressures they exert, while hydrodynamics concerns the motion and flow of fluids, and hydraulics the construction of machines using fluids. But hydrostatics was the name given to apparatus used for demonstrating all effects involving water. Some of these were very attractive. Diving bells were made, containing a tiny human figure; the Cartesian diver could be made to move up and down in a column of water by pressing a membrane over the top of the container; the so-called Tantalus cup demonstrated the effect of a syphon, again sometimes using a human figure. There was a great deal of interest in the eighteenth century in using water for ornamental purposes in elaborate fountains, and there exist glass, or brass, demonstration pieces. Another common piece of equipment was a series of thin glass tubes in a frame to show capillary attraction. More practical were the instruments devised to measure the specific gravity of liquids and solids respectively, the hydrometer, or areometer, and the gravimeter. Hydrometers were

extensively used by brewers and excise officers, and there are many available to collectors. The Clarke pattern dates from 1730, and the more accurate design of Sikes was introduced by Act of Parliament in 1817. This was the most popular excise officer's instrument, and can be found in its box, accompanied by a thermometer, glass flask, sliding computing scale, and tables. Hydrometers for specific gravities greater than water, for acids and alkalies, were sold by William Twaddell of Glasgow from about 1800.

Electricity

The word electricity derives from the Greek word for amber, since the Greeks were aware of the attractive quality of rubbed amber. But it was not until the eighteenth century that the effects of frictional electricity began to be seriously studied. Hauksbee produced the first 'frictional electrical machine', consisting of a round glass globe, revolved by a handle, with a pad of leather pressed against it. In dry conditions, electricity can be generated by the rubbing on the surface of the glass. Later versions of the frictional electrical machine were a cylinder of glass—this type was patented by Edward Nairne in 1784 as a 'medical electrical machine'—and the plate machine, consisting of discs of glass, spun between two pairs of rubbing cushions. These discs were occasionally made up to 6 feet (1.8 m) in diameter for demonstration machines intended to produce dramatic effects, but the most common type of plate machine had a diameter of between 1 and $1\frac{1}{2}$ feet (30–45 cm). The plate machine should not be confused with the later 'Wimshurst induction machine', which is distinguished by having oblongs of metal foil round the edge of the glass discs.

Following the invention of the frictional electrical machine, the most important development was the invention in 1745 by von Kleist in Germany, and Musschenbroek in Leyden of the Leyden jar, which condensed the electric charge and allowed much greater sparks to be produced. These are glass jars of varying size, covered with foil, and with a conductor through the cork in the neck. These can be found today, as can the insulating stools used in demonstrations, which have glass legs. Some of the intriguing demonstration equipment to be used for demonstrating frictional electricity can sometimes be found. This includes carved heads with human hair, intended to be made to stand on end by the electric charge; the 'gamut of bells' which consisted of eight bells on a stand linked by an electric whirl carrying a clapper that, in revolving, strikes each bell in turn; the 'thunder house', intended to show the

131

need for a continuous metallic lightning conductor, by having an explosion caused by a tiny charge of gunpowder, set off at the point of discontinuity by an electric charge. Current electricity was first worked on in 1790 by Luigi Galvani, professor of anatomy at Bologna. He was followed by Alexander Volta of Pavia who at the beginning of the nineteenth century developed a current generating device which became known as Volta's pile, or the Voltaic pile.

Heat and Meteorology

One of the earliest of demonstration pieces concerned with heat is 's Gravesande's ball and ring, which shows that metal expands when heated. The metal ball will pass through the ring when cold, but will not do so when heated. Pairs of large, brass parabolic mirrors were used to show that heat could be focused from one to another, just as light is focused. Other demonstration apparatus showing the effects of heat includes the thermoscope, devised by Galileo, using a column of water in a spiral glass tube which rose as air in a bulb expanded with heat; and the pulse glass which consists of two glass bulbs linked by a tube containing coloured spirit; when one bulb is held in the hand, the warmth causes the spirit to boil and flow into the other bulb. A late nineteenth century heat device was Crookes' radiometer, consisting of a glass bulb, containing discs of mica mounted on four pivoted arms. These discs are coloured white on one side, and black on the other. When placed in the sun, or near a light source, the black surfaces, absorbing and emitting heat readily, cause the device to revolve rapidly.

Thermometer

The thermometer, a descendant of Galileo's thermoscope, is used to measure temperature. The problems in making thermometers were to find a substance which would respond uniformly to changes in temperature, and to devise a suitable scale for measurement. Daniel Fahrenheit of Amsterdam, working in the early years of the eighteenth century, was the first maker to produce thermometers of any accuracy. He used mercury for the first time in 1717. It proved much more satisfactory than alcohol, though it was technically more difficult to use. It has a more uniform expansion rate, and a far wider temperature range than alcohol. Fahrenheit also worked on producing a satisfactory scale. The scale he made in 1724 had three fixed points: 0° was the freezing point of a mixture of ammonium chloride and snow, 32° was the freezing point of water, and 96° the mouth temperature of a healthy human being. This Fahrenheit scale was used on the majority of English thermometers of the eighteenth century.

Many other scales were devised at about the same time, but only two are important, those of the French physicist René de Réaumur and Anders Celsius, a Swedish astronomer; these are generally found on Continental-made instruments. The Réaumur scale had only one fixed point, the freezing point of water 0°, and it rose to 80° (the boiling point of water). Réaumur used alcohol in his thermometers. The Celsius scale is remarkable in that it was the first to consist of 100 degrees. It had the boiling point of water at 0° and freezing at 100°. The year after it was produced in 1742, the Celsius scale was inverted by Cristin of Lyons, into what has been known successively as the Lyonnais scale and the centigrade scale. Today we are reverting to the name Celsius.

There are thermometers made for a huge variety of specialised purposes, from cooking to mining. Early thermometers usually have scale plates of brass, often silvered, and cases of mahogany. More modern thermometers have ivory or boxwood plates, and softwood cases. The maximum and minimum thermometer was devised by James Six of Colchester at the end of the eighteenth century. It uses an alcohol thermometer to push a column of mercury, which, in turn, pushes steel indices into place to record maximum and minimum temperatures.

Hygrometer

The hygrometer is intended to demonstrate the humidity of the air. In the eighteenth century, the way this was done was by a method first devised in 1663 by Robert Hooke, using the beard of a wild oat. The beard is a tiny spiral which unwinds as the tail becomes damp, and this effect is recorded on a dial by attaching an indicator of straw to the oat-beard. This type of hygrometer is often found associated with barometers after 1760. Occasionally, cat-gut is used instead of the oat-beard. In 1820, a more scientific method of measuring humidity was devised by J. F. Daniell. His hygrometer consisted of a U-shaped glass tube with bulbs at each end, one painted black, the other covered with silk. The tube contains ether, and there are thermometers inside the tube and mounted on the pillar supporting the tube. Ether dropped on the silk surrounding one of the bulbs evaporates, and the consequent cooling causes dew to form on the surface of the other bulb. The temperature at which this occurs establishes the 'dew-point'. Later versions of the hygrometer were all developments of Daniell's principle.

Barometer

The barometer is designed to measure the pressure or weight of the air. At sea level this is 15 psi (1 kg/cm^2), and this has significance in the scientific study of the air and gases, but the general popularity of the barometer stems from the seventeenth-century discovery of the connection between alterations in the pressure of the air and changes in the weather. In its simplest form, a barometer consists of a glass tube under 3 feet (c. 1 m) in length, sealed at its upper end. The sealed end of the tube contains a vacuum, below which is a column of mercury. The open end of the tube stands in a cistern filled with mercury. An alternative is to have a bent or siphon tube, with the shorter leg open. The pressure of the air on the surface of the mercury in the cistern, or the open end of the siphon tube, is recorded by the rise and fall of the mercury at the top of the tube. A further development was to have the tube bent at an angle of just over 90°, so that the movement of the mercury was magnified, and therefore easier to measure.

Most eighteenth-century barometers are of the stick type, that is, the tube is held in a long, narrow mahogany case, frequently with some kind of ornamental top. Others are of the bent tube type, some with a mirror set within the angle, in a picture-frame mounting. A third type, invented in the 1660s, was the wheel barometer, which uses a siphon tube with a float on the mercury and a pulley and weight arrangement to record rises and falls of the mercury on a circular dial. This type of barometer, in which the tube is invisible, did not become popular until the early nineteenth century, when it was the arrangement used in the very common banjo barometers. Barometers were often associated with thermometers and hygrometers, and many also incorporated a vernier scale for greater accuracy of measurement; they can also be found associated with clocks.

The first instrument maker to specialise in the manufacture of barometers was John Patrick, who was described in the *Lexicon Technicum* of 1704 as the 'Torricellian Operator'. This title commemorates Evangelista Torricelli, to whom the invention of the barometer in 1644 is generally ascribed. Patrick was sufficiently well-known to have been visited in 1710 by the German traveller and diarist, von Uffenbach, who called him 'an optico and weather-glass maker'. Patrick published two pamphlets on meteorological topics, publicising his products. The most sought-after of antique barometers are probably those made by Daniel Quare, a Quaker clock-maker of London at the beginning of the eighteenth century. His superb instruments, made of ivory, silver and fine woods, fetch thousands of pounds in sale-rooms. Any genuine eighteenth-century or Regency barometer is likely to command a high price today.

Most antique barometers will have had replacement tubes and mercury, because the tubes are very easily broken in transit by careless handling of the heavy, liquid metal. Late Victorian and Edwardian stick and banjo barometers can be very like the earlier examples, but elaborate, Gothic decoration may indicate their late date. Barometers dating from the latter half of the nineteenth century may also have an aneroid barometric mechanism in place of the mercury tube; this was patented in 1845 by a Frenchman, Lucien Vidie. The mechanism consists of a metal bellows, partly evacuated of air, which is very sensitive to changes in air pressure that are recorded by a pointer over a circular dial. In the first half of the nineteenth century, an extensive trade in London-made, banjo barometers began to be conducted by Italians, who retailed them in hundreds of British towns and cities. These instruments, usually carrying a level, dial, and hygrometer (sometimes a thermometer as well), bear the name of an Italian tradesman, incongruously linked to an English place-name. One of the most famous of these firms, which still exists, was Negretti & Zambra, which became a very considerable supplier of all sorts of scientific instruments, especially meteorological ones.

The *Baromètre liègeois* is a foreteller of storms and is thought to have evolved from drinking vessels for birds. It is a pear-shaped, closed glass vessel with a long spout rising from the bottom. When the vessel is half filled with water, changes in the atmospheric pressure will cause the water level in the spout to rise for a storm (low pressure), or lower for fine weather (high pressure). During the early eighteenth century, glass blowers of Liège produced these domestic weather indicators, and they have been copied and simplified up to the beginning of the twentieth century. They are not infrequently met with in the Netherlands today. Naturally, being of glass, they are difficult to date, but later ones may have the retailer's name etched on.

Spectroscope
In its various forms, the spectroscope has contributed more to modern science than perhaps any other instrument. It is the oldest optical method of chemical analysis, and is the sole means for discovering the nature and composition of the stars. The year 1860 saw the start of chemical analysis by this means, as proposed by Bunsen and Kirchhoff

in Germany.

The basic features are a slit and collimator for producing a parallel beam of light, a prism or grating for dispersing the different wavelengths, and a telescope for observing the dispersed spectrum. Spectroscopes from the late nineteenth and early twentieth centuries do come on the market from schools and laboratories. Principal early makers were John Browning and Adam Hilger in London, and Schmidt & Haensch of Berlin.

7
Weights and Measures

Systems of weighing and measuring date from the establishment of settled, civilised communities, which practised barter and trade. The exchange of goods requires agreement on the amount or mass of the goods offered by each party, in order to assess their equality. There is evidence, much of it pictorial, that men were using weights and scales, capacity measures, and linear measuring rods, from at least 3000 B.C. At first, each village or market place had its own standards of weights and measures, and different ones were used for different goods. The latter custom has persisted into this century with the use of troy weight, a different metrological scale from avoirdupois (the commonly-known Imperial weight scale), for precious metals and pharmaceuticals. Only when there existed a strong, centralised government were attempts made at standardisation. The Romans, for example, had only one standard weight unit, the *libra*. All through the Middle Ages, a vast and bewildering variety of weights and measures existed, undoubtedly making commerce more difficult. Despite frequent attempts by governments—edicts of Charlemagne, Magna Carta—regional differences persisted within different countries. It was the introduction of the metric-decimal system by the Revolutionary government of France in 1792 which was the first really effective step towards national standardisation. In the course of the nineteenth century, most countries adopted and standardised to either the metric system, or the Imperial (British) system. In this century, we are at last struggling through to the adoption of the metric system internationally.

Early civilisations, such as the Egyptian and the pre-mediaeval Islamic, achieved a remarkable degree of accuracy in their weights. Obviously, the weighing of precious metals, coinage, and drugs required strict control to prevent fraud, so most governments introduced methods of certification. This involved the stamping of weighing equipment with city or state symbols. In addition, in mediaeval Europe, makers of weights put their own stamps, or mastersigns, on the weights, as a guarantee of accuracy.

Types of antique scales which may be found by collectors vary from large steelyards used for weighing sacks of grain to the delicate balances used for weighing coins or drugs. Steelyards or extended spring scales were generally used for heavy loads. Domestic scales of the Victorian and Edwardian periods are of the spring type, with brass, or tin pans resting on a cross-shaped support. Letter scales, very common throughout the nineteenth and early twentieth centuries, were either balances, or spring scales, or sometimes of the self-indicating type. The accuracy of the balance was required for weighing coins, jewels, and chemicals. Chemical balances, for laboratory use, which are of very fine workmanship, are found in their own fitted cases. Favourites with collectors are coin balances, and the small, portable balances in cases which were used for all private weighing purposes during the Victorian period.

Balances and Scales

The Balance This is the most accurate weighing mechanism and consists of two pans suspended from the ends of a beam, which is supported at its mid-point. One pan is used for the goods to be weighed, the other for the weights. Equilibrium of the loads is indicated by an exactly horizontal position of the beam. At first, the equilibrium was judged by eye, but later balances all incorporated an indicator or pointer to show the equilibrium, or lack of it.

The Bismar and Steelyard These are the two types of scales using the principle of the lever, with unequal arms for the beam. All scales with unequal arms use a single counterpoise, fitting only one specific scale. There are two methods of weighing with an unequal-arm beam. In the bismar, the counterpoise is fixed to one end of the beam, and the axis of the beam can be shifted quite simply, for example, by a loose loop of cord supporting the beam that can be moved along it. As soon as the beam is horizontal, showing that equilibrium has been reached, the correct weight can be read off the scale marked on the beam from the position of the cord loop (the fulcrum). Bismars made in Russia, Finland, and Sweden in the eighteenth and nineteenth centuries can be found today.

Steelyards are levers with an immovable axis or fulcrum, which have a pan or hook attached to the shorter arm for holding the load, and, suspended from the longer arm, a movable counterpoise. At the place where the counterpoise keeps the beam exactly horizontal, the weight of the object is indicated on a scale, again marked on the beam. The steelyard was extremely common, and still remains in occasional use.

Self-indicating Scales These have no beam at all, but consist of one pan or hook for the load on a long arm, with a heavy counterpoise on a short arm. Once the load is in position, the counterpoise swings upwards from its rest position, which is vertically downwards, to balance the load (by the principle of the lever), and an indicator on the long arm points to the inscribed scale, giving the weight of the load.

Spring Scales Unlike those described above, these do not rely on achieving a balance, but are based on the deformation of elastic material by weight. The elastic material is usually a steel coil, which is compressed or extended by the weight of an attached object, the degree of compression or extension being recorded by a pointer on a scale, which has to be calibrated by the maker.

Coin Balances (Money Scales) These are known from the late fifteenth century. The earliest type consisted of a hand-held balance with two pans, which fitted into a small box carved from solid wood with individual sockets for the weights. The earliest weights used with these balances were square, but following a Proclamation of Charles I in 1632, English coin weights were obliged by law to be round. Coin balances from the reign of Charles I are likely to bear his initial, surmounted by a crown, as a verification mark. A boxed balance of the late seventeenth century may have the maker's trade card stuck into the inside of the box lid. During the eighteenth century, a number of new designs for coin balances appeared, for there was a large market in these, brought about by the circulation of many foreign coins in Britain, and indeed all over Europe, with the increase of foreign trade. Anyone doing business needed to have the means of checking gold coins both for the weight of gold, and also for base metal content. For the latter reason, a number of hydrostatical balances were produced, with which a coin's specific gravity could be tested by weighing in air and then in water. One popular coin balance of this period was of the steelyard type, consisting of a slim rule marked with a scale, which could be used on any convenient flat surface, from which hung a clip to hold the coin. This fitted into a pull-apart case. Following the recoinage in the 1770s, and the New Standard of 1774, which withdrew from currency coins below a specified weight, another steelyard type of balance was produced, which 'popped up' when the lid of the slim box was opened. A hinged weight

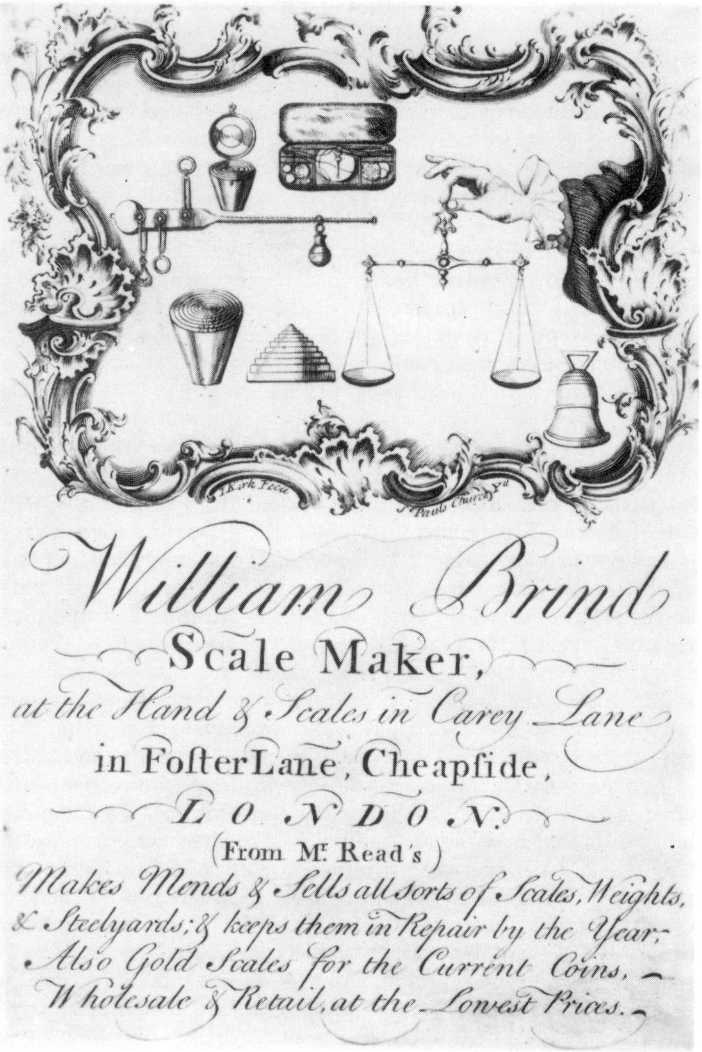

Trade card of William Brind, Foster Lane, c. 1750.

could be swung into two positions for weighing the guinea and half-guinea, a great simplification compared with earlier scales. The design is attributed to Anthony Wilkinson in Lancashire, and various makers' names are found associated with the towns of Kirkby, Ormskirk, Prescot, and Birmingham. In 1817, new coins, the sovereign and half-sovereign, were introduced. To test these coins for wear, and to detect counterfeit coins, the so-called sovereign rocker was invented, a simple little balance in a pull-apart case, which included slot gauges to check the size of the two gold coins. Other designs of coin balance existed, including a spring balance combined with a pen, and a desk-top balance for gold and silver coins. But after 1860, it gradually became less common for the general public to check coins, and the production of coin balances declined.

Alongside the more novel designs described above, the traditional two-pan balances continued in use, their date only indicated by the style of the box. Solid wood boxes, with the slots for the balance and weights carved out, are an indication of considerable age, probably dating from the early eighteenth century. A fishskin-covered box, lined with velvet or silk almost certainly dates from the eighteenth century. The commonest type of box was oval, made of japanned metal, first produced in the mid-eighteenth century, but in use for about a hundred years.

Another way of dating a boxed coin balance is by means of the weights, which may be marked for specific coins. It is then necessary only to find out when the coin was in circulation. In early boxes, there may be individual slots for the weights, so it is easy to see if the weights supplied are original. But with later boxes, there is merely a compartment for all the weights, and it is possible that stray weights may have been added. But sometimes there may be a table of coins and their current weight inside the box lid, which will help to verify the weights, and to date the box. It is, however, common to find an odd assortment of weights, either added over several generations of use, or by modern owners or dealers.

Chinese 'Opium' Scales These very characteristic scales may occasionally be found. The scales have a beam of ivory, with a single brass pan, and they work on the steelyard principle, and are contained in a wooden case made in the shape of a banjo or violin, with the beam running up the narrow part, and the pan contained in the wider portion. The weight is of brass, with a rod through it, to which the suspension cord is attached.

These scales are of Chinese origin, and are also called *dotchin*. They are first referred to in literature in the seventeenth century, and were used for weighing precious metals, jewels, and medicines (with the possible inclusion of opium). They continued in production well into the nineteenth century.

Apothecaries' Balances The distinguishing features are the glass pans (occasionally ivory), and that they are usually hand-held. They were intended for use by doctors, who did their own dispensing, and in the home. Typical accompaniments in the box would be a tiny brass shovel, and a small glass measuring cup.

Jewellers' Balances Always mounted on a stand, these are intended for much more precise work. The balance beam will be very thin and the indicator will be very exact, the pans tiny, and often made of silver.

Chemical Balances By the end of the eighteenth century, these required an extremely high degree of precision, and were masterpieces of the instrument maker's craft. The first attempts at constructing an exact balance for scientific use were made at the beginning of the eighteenth century, and in the following hundred years many of the leading instrument makers of London tried their hand at producing them, including Ramsden and Troughton. Such balances from the eighteenth and nineteenth centuries are not very likely to be found outside museums. They can be recognised by being associated with a glass case, usually with drawers below. The case will usually be mounted on levelling screws, and the front, and possibly the sides, will be movable.

Letter Scales Dating most commonly from the Victorian and Edwardian periods, these are usually of the balance type, made of brass, with a wooden base. The letter rests on a flat rectangular brass plate, the weights on a smaller, circular one. The table of weights and equivalent postage is often inscribed on the rectangular plate.

Grain Scales Examples exist of a special kind of scales known as a chondrometer, the purpose of which, according to an instruction label in an example made by Watkins & Hill in 1826, was 'to ascertain the quality of all kinds of grain or farina by inspection only'. The scale reads off in pounds per bushel (a capacity measure of eight gallons) when the brass cylindrical cup is filled with the sample of grain.

Early English examples date from *c.* 1710. Grain scales exist that were made in Germany, Holland, Sweden, and France during the nineteenth century.

Weights

The earliest weights were simply pieces of hard natural stone of convenient size and shape. Early Egyptian weights that are preserved from about 2500 B.C. are made of granite. Later, bronze and lead were used, but although metal had the advantage of high specific weight so that metal weights could be smaller in volume, there was the problem of corrosion. While the Greeks used lead or bronze for weights, the Romans used stone, often polished serpentine, up until the third century A.D. Glass, having the durable quality of stone, was used in Islamic countries in the mediaeval period, particularly for weights needing high accuracy. In mediaeval Europe, iron and brass, or combinations of the two, were generally used for weights, with the occasional use of other metals, and sometimes glass or glazed clay. By the eighteenth century, brass, iron and pewter were the common materials for weights all over Europe. For standard weights that have to keep their accuracy over long periods rock crystal, bronze, and platinum have been used.

Weights come in a remarkable variety of shapes. The majority are geometric: spheres, hemispheres, squares, cubes, discs, polygon forms. But representational weights are also numerous, and very attractive, coming in the form of animals and even human effigies. Pharmaceutical weights were sometimes made in the form of the symbol used in prescriptions, as an aid to accuracy. Another common construction for weights of all kinds was dictated by convenience: the different denominations were made to fit one inside the other. The simplest way of doing this was to use weights in the form of cups. Perhaps the most famous and sought-after of nested weights are those made in Nuremberg in the seventeenth century. These fitted into a master cup, which was most beautifully embellished, and had a carrying handle. But brass nested weights, because of their convenience, continued to be produced well into this century; they often appear older than, in fact, they are, because of the traditional design.

The symbols and inscriptions on weights are a vast and complex subject, and collectors need to look up the tables of the wide variety of weights in use in different countries at different times. The standard unit in Germany from the twelfth to the nineteenth centuries was the mark, or marc (2 marks = 1 pound = 467 gm), and subdivisions included the loth, the quint and the pfennig. The French pound was the livre (1 livre = 489 gm), and subdivisions included the marc, the once, the gros, the denier and the grain. In England there were two main weight systems, the Troy, generally used for precious metals, precious stones and dispensing drugs, and the avoirdupois, the usual commercial system. In Troy Weight 1 penny weight = 24 grains; 1 ounce = 20 penny weights; 1 pound = 12 ounces (= 373 gm), and 1 pound avoirdupois = 14 ounces 11 penny weights 16 grains. In Avoirdupois Weight 1 dram = $27\frac{1}{3}$ (nearly) grains; 1 ounce = 16 drams; 1 pound = 16 ounces (= 453 gm); 1 pound Troy = 13 ounces 40 grains.

There was also an apothecaries' scale (superseded in 1864) of which 1 scruple = 20 grains; 1 drachm = 3 scruples; 1 ounce = 8 drachms and 1 pound (Troy) = 12 ounces. Notice that it is only the grain that is common to all these scales of weights. 1 lb Troy = 5760 grains, and 1 lb avoirdupois = 7000 grains.

Measures of Length

The earliest units of linear measure were based on approximate body measurements: the fingers and hand, the forearm (cubit), the length of both arms fully extended, measured across the body (fathom), the foot, the stride (giving a mile of 1000 paces), etc. The inch derived from the width of the thumb, as a twelfth part of the foot, while the cubit measured approximately 18 inches (45 cm), or slightly more; the Egyptian royal cubit was 20.6 inches (52 cm). The Greek and Roman foot measured approximately 12 inches (30 cm), and these continued in use throughout Europe until the mediaeval period. In England, a statute of 1305 laid down the standard of linear measure, mainly for the purpose of measuring land. According to this, three grains of dry barley make 1 inch; 12 inches make a foot; three feet make an Ulna, which later was renamed the yard. Henry VII, in 1497, had the first standard yard made, and this octagonal section bronze rod still exists in the Science Museum, London. It is 0.037 inches shorter than the Imperial yard used this century. Elizabeth I, in 1588, confirmed the yard, but added another linear measure, the ell, which measured 45 inches, and was intended as a cloth measure. The ell continued as a legal measure until 1824.

As with weights, so with linear measures, there was the likelihood of very considerable variations from country to country, and also between different towns. The Scottish ell, for example, measured 37 inches, and the Flemish ell 26 to $27\frac{1}{2}$ inches. English-made ell rules for buying continental cloth were therefore made about 27 inches long, while those for the home trade were 37 to 45 inches long. Some ell rules have a variety of different ell lengths marked off.

Yardsticks and ell rules make attractive collectors' items, and can be found from the seventeenth century, though those not in museums are likely to be from the eighteenth and nineteenth centuries. Ell rules are usually made of boxwood, mahogany, or pine with brass ends, and sometimes brass inlay for the scale. Some can be attractively inlaid or carved. Yardsticks again were generally made of wood, but examples exist of metal standard yardsticks, made for use in manorial courts. These are made of brass, usually with a case, and will bear the name of the court, and probably the date and a royal cipher.

Capacity Measures

The so-called 'Winchester Standard' (the association with Winchester dates from Saxon times, when it was the capital city of England) was established by Henry VII in 1497. The measures were defined by the weight in Troy ounces of their contents of wheat, by 'striked measure'; this means with the top levelled off by a spatula or levelling stick. The Winchester measures were declared standard for wheat, wine and ale: a pint $= 12\frac{1}{2}$ Troy ounces of wheat; a quart (2 pints) $= 25$ Troy ounces of wheat; a pottle (4 pints) $= 50$ Troy ounces of wheat; a gallon (8 pints) $= 100$ Troy ounces of wheat and a bushel (64 pints) $= 800$ Troy ounces of wheat.

The original Winchester standard measures for the gallon and the bushel, dating from the fifteenth century, and made of heavy bronze, are to be seen in the Science Museum, London. Standard measures of this type continued to be made until 1824, when the British Imperial measures were established. Standards may still be found dating from the eighteenth and early nineteenth centuries, usually made of brass.

The other historic capacity measure was the wine gallon, which by custom was smaller than the Winchester gallon. Because this caused confusion, it was decided to define the wine gallon in 1707, under an Act of Queen Anne, and this definition was made as 231 cubic inches. By comparison, the Winchester gallon was equivalent to 268 cubic inches, and the Imperial gallon of 1824 to 277 cubic inches. This is the reason why different measures for wine gallons and ale gallons (ale and beer were measured by the Winchester standard) appear on antique measuring equipment. An interesting point is that the Winchester bushel and the Queen Anne wine gallon passed to the United States, and were legally adopted in 1836, where they remained the standards into this century, differing from the British Imperial measures brought in after 1824.

Antique capacity measures made for use in business and in the home, unlike the official standards, were generally made of ash, beech, or oak. Measures for grain and other dry goods were made of thin, steamed bentwood, often banded with iron, and were the work of coopers. Measures for liquids, made by turners, were from hollowed-out solid wood. Alternatives were metal and horn. Nearly all old measures are stamped with the crown and initials of the reigning monarch, and usually with a date. A twentieth century measure may also carry a number, which will be the reference number of the Weights and Measures office which verified it.

What we think of as liquid measures, the gill, pint, quart and gallon, were also, as has been made clear above, used for dry goods, such as grain, peas and beans. So the liquid and dry measures were more or less complementary.

Liquid Measure
4 gills/20 fl. oz = 1 pint
2 pints = 1 quart
4 quarts = 1 gallon

Dry Measure
2 gallons = 1 peck
8 gallons = 1 bushel
64 gallons = 1 quarter

Beer Measure
$4\frac{1}{2}$ gallons = 1 pin
9 gallons = 1 firkin
18 gallons = 1 kilderkin
36 gallons = 1 barrel
54 gallons = 1 hogshead
72 gallons = 1 puncheon
108 gallons = 1 butt

Wine Measure
42 gallons = 1 tierce
63 gallons = 1 hogshead
84 gallons = 1 puncheon
126 gallons = 1 pipe or butt
252 gallons = 1 tun

Makers

By the eighteenth century, scale and balance making was a specialist craft, as is made clear by the trade cards that may be found in some balance boxes. Among these are Henry Neale and William Brind of London, Thomas Beach of Birmingham, and Collet Frères of Paris. A particularly skilled and important maker was R. B. Bate of London, who was a specialist metrologist, making hydrometers and saccharometers for the Customs and Excise, and the standard weights and measures after 1824 when Imperial standards were brought in. Another specialist firm of high reputation was Richard Vandome & Co., who made standards for the Bank of England and the East India Company. Another name that appears on a number of standard measures of length and capacity, and also on weights, is that of de Grave of London, who was working in the first half of the nineteenth century. After Charles de Grave died, his widow, Mary, continued to run the business, signing herself 'Mary de Grave, widow of Chas. de Grave'.

8
Medical Instruments

Medicine was thoroughly based on the teaching of Galen, the Greek physician, until the eighteenth century. Doctors had to find out how the four humours were out of balance in their patient, and then set about restoring the balance, a process that often involved copious bleeding or change of diet. The four humours were melancholy, choler, phlegm and blood. This purely conceptual scheme had no possibility for profitable experimental study. Changed attitudes during the development of the scientific revolution in the eighteenth century gave rise to the enormous increase in medical understanding during the nineteenth. Here the improved microscopes after 1830 played an important part.

Surgery, on the other hand, was practised from very early times, and is essentially practical. The name comes from the French *chirurgie* which is from the Greek, meaning 'hand-work'. Instruments were essential, and surgical instruments found in the ruins of the Italian city of Pompeii, which was wrecked by an eruption of Vesuvius in 79 B.C., are quite remarkably modern in appearance. But then the human body has not changed, and scalpels and saws are the constant stock-in-trade. Surgeons were needed on the battle-field, so it is hardly surprising that mediaeval makers of instruments were the armourers. New forms of wounds—gun-shot rather than blade—required new methods. The bow saw (like a modern hacksaw) and the tenon saw, which derive from Roman times, evolved according to the type of amputation. From the sixteenth century, Continental craftsmen enriched the saws with decorated iron parts, and handles of ivory, fishskin, or fine woods. The seventeenth century witnessed improvements in surgery along with the new attitudes to science. An influence here was Richard Wiseman, said to be the 'father of English Surgery', who died in 1676 after service to Charles II in exile on the Continent, and later James II. He encouraged primary amputations, before the onset of fever. By the end of the eighteenth century, serious attention had been paid to design, and lighter saws with cross-hatched, ebony handles for better grip were made.

Throughout Europe, surgery improved greatly during the eighteenth century, and teaching colleges were set up in Paris, Vienna, Berlin, and Edinburgh. In London, there were private schools, notably William Hunter's. The Royal College of Surgeons of London was not founded until 1800. All this activity naturally generated a demand for instruments, and this was met by the cutlers. The barber-surgeon connection is reflected again in the production of razors and scissors, lancets, and fleams. The trade in surgical instruments is quite separate from other scientific instruments.

Of course, there are a very great number of surgical instruments, and many types have variations in size and material, and have variations according to the particular part of the anatomy they have to deal with. For a detailed study of the subject of surgical instruments it is necessary to acquire a trade catalogue, late Victorian or Edwardian, which illustrates most of the variations.

A considerable manufacturer and retailer of surgical instruments is the firm of Weiss, still in operation from 1787. Towards the end of the nineteenth century, Down Bros., had a large factory in London. Both companies published extensive catalogues that are most instructive.

Surgical Instruments

The Napoleonic Wars created a demand for surgeons' kits, consequently cases of instruments may be found from this time. Such kits are probably in red-lined mahogany boxes. By the early twentieth century, amputation sets are in brassbound mahogany cases, and consist of a large saw (tenon saw type), a finger saw, Hey's skull saw, large and small amputation knives, scalpels, artery forceps, bullet forceps, catheters, gun-shot probe, ligature silk, needles, tourniquets. In 1930 such a set retailed for between £11 to £15, depending on the range of instruments included. Sir William Hey designed his small-bladed skull saws in 1803 while working at the Leeds infirmary, and every kit has included one or more ever since. Large numbers of kits will have been sold to army and navy surgeons, and to those employed on passenger ships. Being the property of the surgeon himself, some will have survived to reach the collectors' market.

Trepanning is held to be even older than amputation. Neolithic skeletons have been found with holes bored in the skull, presumably done with flint knives. Reasons for head-boring include the release of demons causing headaches or epilepsy on the one hand, and release of a depression or fracture from a blow on the other. It is recorded that

William, Prince of Orange, in the sixteenth century, was trepanned seventeen times for the relief of migraine.

There is often confusion in the name of the instrument. A trepan is a surgical instrument in the form of a crown saw, an iron cone with teeth filed into the lower rim. A trephine is also a crown saw, but represents a later form, after about 1630, which has a centre pin to guide and steady the instrument. Trepanation is an operation with the trepan, and trephination with the trephine. Trepanning is nowadays also an engineering term, when a core of earth is removed.

Cased sets of trephines include a hand tool and four to six different sized crown saws that are interchangeable. Tools look either like a cork-screw, with a cross handle, or like a carpenter's brace. Forceps, drills, and other perforators will probably be included. Elevators are another necessary tool for lifting portions of fractured skull; they look rather like manicure implements. Most kits available today are eighteenth- and nineteenth-century, but it must be remembered that twentieth-century kits are also obtainable.

Bloodletting Instruments

Phlebotomy signifies blood-letting, literally from the Greek, vein-cutting. It is particularly important in the four humour theory of Galen, and it became a general all-embracing 'cure' (often far from it), but was not to be done when the moon was on the wane, or during a South wind. The lancet is the instrument used for blood-letting, and sets can often be very attractive, each blade protected in ivory or tortoise-shell, all held in silver or fish-skin cases. The blade is double sided, with a sharp point. A fleam is a lancet where the pointed blade is at right-angles to the shaft, rather like a hatchet. The name can also refer to a lancet for bleeding horses. A scarificator is the name given to an instrument that makes several incisions at the same time. A small brass box holds four to twelve razor-sharp, curved blades that are retracted below the slotted surface of the instrument and then released by a trigger. The blades flash out to give a depth of cut governed by a turn-screw. (They must be handled with extreme caution.) Most scarificators found today are nineteenth-century, but it must be borne in mind that they were still offered for sale in 1900. At that date a set of two, one with twelve blades and one with four to be used on the temple, together with six cupping glasses, and a spirit lamp, all in a brass-bound, mahogany case, retailed for £3 10s (£3.50p).

The cupping glass is a small, glass bell-jar, which is placed over the

Trade card of Henry Patten, Holborn, c. 1750.

wound caused by the lancet or scarificator to draw out and to collect the blood. The ability to draw the blood is obtained by heating the air in the glass before applying it to the skin. On cooling a vacuum is produced, which readily sucks the blood from the wound. Cupping glasses may be found with a brass collar at the closed end and an attachment for an exhausting syringe. Here the air can be pumped out of the little bell-jar, and this new technique of obtaining a vacuum can be traced to the experimental philosophers of about 1710.

Catheters

This is a thin tube (probably of silver) for passing into the bladder. It is used to remove urine from the bladder, or to apply solutions to alleviate strictures or ulcers. The Romans used such an instrument. Catheters for men normally come in cased sets of twelve of different gauge. They are about 12 inches (30 cm) long, with a curved end which is perforated. For the female, they are shorter, wider, and straight.

Lithotomy Instruments

These are for removing bladder stones which form in the bladder as a result of a poor and monotonous diet, and the operation to remove a stone is centuries old. Many instruments were devised to grasp and extract the stone through an incision. In the first half of the nineteenth century tools were devised to crush the stone while still in the bladder.

Obstetric Instruments

These were devised in mediaeval Europe for use by midwives. Because no man was allowed at a birth, no doctor could at that time be present. Things altered after about 1650, first in France and then in Britain. Peter Chamberlen, a Huguenot descendant, is known to have used forceps in the middle of the century. The trade secret came out eventually, and during the eighteenth century many improvements were made. The forceps have large blades, with cut-away centres and curved ends, to grasp the head of the child.

Post Mortem Instruments

These are similar to amputation sets, but include a combined mallet and hatchet, plus a chisel.

Diagnostic Aids

Diagnostic aids are readily available, the hammer, called a percussor (it may not be recognised for what it is), and the ubiquitous stethoscope. In medical terms, percussion is the act of striking with one finger or with a small hammer against another finger placed on the surface of the body. The sound produced tells the doctor the physical state of that part of the body. The monaural stethoscope was invented by the French physician, René Laennec in 1816. His treatise of 1819 was not translated into English until 1825. About 12 inches (30 cm) long, with a wide rim at one end (for the ear), they are made of fine woods, ivory, pewter or silver. The familiar binaural stethoscope was patented in 1855 by G. P. Caniman of New York. It must not be thought that the new type ousted the single-tube type; they were sold in 1900 scarcely changed over the years, and they are still used today in maternity cases.

Medicine Chests

The apothecaries prepared and sold drugs and medicines, and the London Livery Company had the right to license medical practitioners. Physicians would need to have their own stock of preparations because of difficulties of travel in rural areas, and some larger households would also have their medicine chest. These can be most attractive, with the finely made bottles in a red-lined mahogany chest. Perhaps a pestle and mortar, a simple balance with weights (see Chapter 7), and measuring flasks are included. Some of the medicines for the household are likely to be emetic tartar, spirits of lavender, laudanum, milk of sulphur, bark, tincture of myrrh, basilicon, Rochelle salts, magnesia, spirits of hartshorn, pile ointment and linament. Savory & Moore is a well-known Bond Street firm that has provided medicines and drugs from the 1790s to the present day.

Dental Instruments

Dentistry was still not a recognised branch of medicine until the mid-nineteenth century. Although Barber-Surgeons will have been willing to attend to teeth, the minor operation of extracting teeth is an easy one, and fell into the province of fair-ground tooth-drawers and even blacksmiths. The mediaeval instrument was the 'Pelican', named after its appearance. Its two parts could lock round a tooth and tighten as leverage was applied. It was replaced by the tooth-key, invented in England in 1742, and called on the Continent the 'clef anglais'. Early ones had a handle and a shaft just like a key of the period; at the end was a claw projecting to one side, which could grip as the key was twisted. In the nineteenth century these were superseded by the dental forceps. These are like nippers, with crooked and cleft blades. The forms vary for the left and right side of the mouth, for the different teeth, and for children and adults. Although superseded, the tooth-key was still offered for sale in 1900, but with an ebony handle like a cork-screw. Treatment to the teeth, as opposed to removal, was rare in Britain until the Dental Society was founded in 1856. The bow-drill had been used in the eighteenth century, and George Washington's dentist, John Greenwood of Boston, used a spinning wheel to drive a drill. By the 1860s, the motorised dental drill had been brought into use.

Sets of forceps and of drills exist. Included in them will be many other implements for special jobs, such as extracting roots, scaling, applying fillings, files and, of course, the dental mirror. The 1908 catalogue of the dental supplier, Claudius Ash, Sons & Co., Ltd., who had branches all over Europe, ran to nearly 1,000 pages.

Ophthalmology and Medical Electrics

Other medical matters give rise to instruments. In ophthalmology eye-testing kits and lenses in spectacles are made by optical instrument makers who may also produce microscopes and telescopes. A medical electrical machine was patented in 1782 by Edward Nairne, the famous scientific instrument maker. It was for administering electric shocks, which were thought to be beneficial for a number of ailments. In Victorian times the machine used was an induction coil, where the electrical tension was generated by turning a handle. Such devices are frequently met with today.

9
Practical Advice on Collecting

Advice on Identification

If you have some antique instrument that you have difficulty in identifying, it is possible to seek advice from a museum. Museum staff are not allowed to value objects, but they are always helpful over identification and dating; if they themselves cannot help, they can refer the problem to someone else with the required expertise. It is always wiser to write for an appointment, rather than call at a museum unannounced. When writing to a museum, always send a photograph of the object to be identified, and a stamped addressed envelope. Another source of identification, and valuation as well, is an auction room. The leading auction rooms can usually help, if sent a detailed description and a good photograph of the object. Sotheby's, Christie's, and Phillips' all deal in scientific instruments, and could help in this way.

Dating

Age and rarity are, of course, the most significant factors in establishing the value of an antique scientific instrument, but these are by no means the only factors; others to take into account are condition, completeness, current tastes in collecting, and historical significance.

The simplest means of establishing the age of an instrument is to find a date inscribed on it. In a few cases, there may be the risk of forgery, and, if a date only is to be found, it should be examined carefully for possible alteration, and for compatibility of style with the period. A date associated with the maker's signature is the most satisfactory form of dating. When a signature and date appear on an instrument, it is interesting to consult a reliable reference work (see bibliography), to discover such details as are known about the maker. In the Victorian period, and later, the name may well be that of a retailer rather than the maker, since quantity production began to get under way in the early nineteenth century, and even before. A maker's name, associated with a date in the eighteenth century or earlier, may make the instrument of particular historical interest, and it would be worth consulting a specialist museum (see the list on p. 163).

Many instruments bear the name of a maker, without any date. Here the use of a reference book can help to give a date span. It is important to remember that a number of the leading firms of instrument makers were in business for long periods. The Adams family spanned nearly 100 years; the firm of Dollond was operating from the 1750s to the early twentieth century. So a microscope signed 'Dollond' should not immediately be thought to date from the eighteenth century; it may well be late nineteenth. The form of the signature, and the type of lettering used can also give clues as to date to the expert. If the maker worked in London, the form of the address can help with dating. From 1767, numbers replaced signs which originally identified workshops and business premises. Benjamin Martin's address in 1767 was given for the first time as 171 Fleet Street. In 1857, ten London postal districts were designated (S.W., E.C., etc). In 1912, numbers were added to the letters (S.W.10, E.C.4, etc).

Apart from an actual inscription on the instrument, there may be a trade label associated with it in some way; for example, in the box of a microscope. These trade cards and labels are of considerable interest, often being embellished with a selection of the maker's stock in trade, and also with his shop sign. Edmund Culpeper, for example, had his business at the sign of the Crossed Daggers, and this appears on his trade card.

Sometimes, other documents are associated with an instrument, such as instruction leaflets, or other advertising material; or perhaps some note or letter giving provenance. In some cases, these can be of very great interest, though there is, of course, scope for error and substitution. This again is a matter on which advice can be sought from a museum.

Because they provide a means of dating, signatures almost invariably add to the value of instruments. Certain signatures are particularly important, as belonging to makers of high repute; for example, James Short on telescopes; Edward Troughton on astronomical instruments; Ramsden on sextants; Powell & Lealand, or Ploessl of Vienna, on microscopes.

Dating an instrument without the aid of an inscribed date or maker's signature or label is a matter of studying style, materials, and details of workmanship, as well as of knowing something of the history and development of the particular instrument in question. Careful examination of the photographs in this book, as well as visits to museum collec-

156

tions, will help to create the feel for different periods. The brief accounts of the history of a wide range of instruments given in the foregoing chapters will provide at least an introduction to the broad outlines of development.

Materials

The expert's ability to ascribe an antique object to a particular period is built up from observation of all sorts of details: shape, material, decoration, as well as such minutiae as screws, key escutcheons, handles, catches, hinges, box lining material, and so on. This kind of knowledge is largely the result of long experience, but some basic guidelines can be provided.

Many scientific instruments are made wholly or partly from wood, or else they have a container or carrying-case of wood. Very broadly-speaking, the use of mahogany indicates that the object was made later than the beginning of the Georgian period. Mahogany began to be imported from the West Indies at the beginning of the eighteenth century, and the tariff on it was greatly reduced in 1733, making its use common in fine cabinet-making. Prior to this, oak, walnut or fruit woods were used. But the arrival of mahogany, at first imported from Cuba and Jamaica, did not preclude the use of oak and other European woods. In the late nineteenth century, African mahogany came into extensive use; it is considerably lighter in colour than the American wood.

It is almost impossible to date brass, even with modern laboratory techniques, because it is an extremely variable alloy, mainly of copper and zinc, though other elements such as tin may be present in small quantities. With a brass instrument, methods of construction and design have to be relied upon to give clues as to date. Even with instruments made wholly of silver, it is extremely rare to find any hallmark, however fine the quality. Silver is often tarnished black by sulphur in the atmosphere, and may not be readily recognised. But careful cleaning with non-abrasive material of a small portion will establish what the metal is. Sometimes a fine layer of gold has been applied over silver or copper. In old instruments, some of the gilding may well have worn off, and any cleaning must be done with great care.

Pasteboard covered with various types of leather was used on tele-scope and microscope tubes until about 1750, and is also found on instrument boxes. The leather is frequently tooled or stamped in gold leaf. The tooling can provide clues as to country of origin and date, a technique resulting from careful study of the various designs. Shagreen is the name given to the skin of the sting-ray with scales ground flat, and the surface polished and dyed. This extremely hard material was used on microscope and telescope tubes up until the late eighteenth century. It continued in use for boxes of various kinds, particularly for toilet sets, until the mid-twentieth century. In the eighteenth and early nineteenth centuries, sharkskin, invariably dyed black, and rough to the touch in one direction, was used to make cases and boxes for instruments.

It is possible to identify elephant ivory by the 'growth rings' observable in cross-section. Ivory is very hard and impervious, and is almost impossible to date. It was much used for microscope slides, and the screw barrels and handles of simple microscopes in the eighteenth century. In Victorian times, slides were often made of bone, in the interests of cheapness. Bone is not as white, and often has tiny dark flecks in the surface. Ivory is sometimes stained black in eighteenth century instruments, and may be mistaken at first sight for ebony. Cheap wood, such as pine, was sometimes 'ebonised', or dyed black, again for cheapness, and used to make the box-foot of an eighteenth century microscope. In 1846, the process of 'vulcanising' was patented; this involved heat-treating rubber with sulphur to make it very hard. This material was called either vulcanite or ebonite. Again, it may be mistaken for ebony, but on close inspection will be seen to have no grain. With age, it frequently goes matt in appearance.

The fabric with which boxes are lined can often provide a clue as to country of origin and date, though it is unwise to place too much reliance on this. Silk, especially watered silk, was often used in France; scarcely ever in England. A chamois-leather lining is often found in boxes of instruments made in Germany. Eighteenth-century English instruments most frequently had cases lined with green baize or green velvet. Blue and claret are often found in the mahogany boxes of Victorian and Edwardian instruments.

The style of lock and key on an instrument case can often provide help in dating the instrument. Keys made in the eighteenth century can be distinguished by the thin, bow-shaped handle, developed from a crude twist of wire. Early keys usually have the leading edge of the bit cut away to pass the wards of the lock. After the lever lock was invented in 1778, the cuts are found on the bottom edge of the bit. If a box or case has a Bramah lock, this dates it to post-1784, when Joseph Bramah patented his design. Bramah locks are still made today; the key has a tiny, uncut bit, and is castellated at the end of the barrel.

Conservation

The basic principle in caring for antiques of all kinds is to interfere with them as little as possible until you have found out from an expert how to carry out repairs or renovations properly. Do not use abrasive cleaners; be particularly careful about cleaning brass and other metals too vigorously, as you will remove the original lacquer; re-lacquering will give too modern an appearance. It is wise to wear gloves when handling old brass instruments because of the risk of 'finger-etching', which results from the salts in the skin reacting with the metal, and can cause lasting damage. Wooden instruments, or their boxes, that have been kept in a dry, heated atmosphere often come unglued. The old glue should then be carefully removed, and fresh animal or fish glue used in its place. The common sticky tapes should never be used for temporary repairs, as they can remove surfaces, and will eventually degrade.

Bibliography

Banfield, Edwin, *Antique Barometers: An Illustrated Survey* (Hereford, Wayland Publications, 1976)

Bedini, Silvio A., *Early American Scientific Instruments and their Makers* (Washington, D.C., Smithsonian Institution, 1964)

Bedini, Silvio A., *Thinkers and Tinkers: Early American Men of Science* (New York, Charles Scribner's Sons, 1975)

Bennion, Elisabeth, *Antique Medical Instruments* (London, Sotheby Parke Bernet, 1978)

Bion, Nicolas, *The Construction and Principal Uses of Mathematical Instruments* (translated by Edmund Stone, London, 1758; reprinted, Holland Press, 1972)

Bonelli, Maria Luisa Righini, *Il Museo di Storia della Scienza a Firenze* (Milan, Electa Editrice, 1968)

Bracegirdle, Brian, *A History of Microtechnique: The Development of the Microtome and the Development of Tissue Preparation* (London, Heinemann, 1978)

Bradbury, S., *The Evolution of the Microscope* (Oxford, Pergamon Press, 1967)

Brown, Joyce, *Mathematical Instrument-Makers in the Grocers' Company 1688–1800* (London, The Science Museum, 1979)

Ceram, C. W., *Archaeology of the Cinema* (London, Thames & Hudson, 1965)

Cohen, I. Bernard, *Some Early Tools of American Science* (Cambridge, Mass., Harvard University Press, 1950)

Crawforth, Michael A., *Weighing Coins: English Folding Gold Balances of the 18th and 19th Centuries* (London, Cape Horn Trading Coy. Ltd., 1979)

Curtis, Tony, editor, *The Lyle Official Antiques Review* (Galashiels, Lyle Publications, published annually)

Daumas, Maurice, *Scientific Instruments of the 17th and 18th Centuries and their Makers* (London, Batsford, 1972)

Engberts, E., *Descriptive Catalogue of Telescopes in the National Museum of the History of Science, Leyden* (Leyden, 1970)

Frison, Edward, *Henri van Heurck Museum: Geillustreerde Inventaris van de Historische Microscopen Onderdelen en Uitrusting* (Antwerp, Koninklijke Maatschappij voor Dierkunde van Antwerpen, 1966) printed in Dutch, French, German and English

Goodison, Nicholas, *English Barometers 1680–1860: A History of Domestic Barometers and their Makers and Retailers* (Woodbridge, Antique Collectors' Club, 1977)

Guye, Samuel, and Michel, Henri, *Time & Space: Measuring Instruments from the 15th to the 19th Century* (London, Pall Mall Press, 1971)

Hackmann, W. D., *Electricity from Glass: the History of the Frictional Electrical Machine 1600–1850* (Alphen aan den Rijn, Sijthoff and Noordhoff, 1978)

Herbert, A. P., *Sundials Old and New, or Fun with the Sun* (London, Methuen, 1967)

Horský, Zdeněk, and Škopová, Otilie, *Astronomy Gnomonics: A Catalogue of Instruments of the 15th to the 19th Centuries in the Collections of the National Technical Museum, Prague* (Prague, 1968)

King, Henry C., and Millburn, J. R., *Geared to the Stars: the Evolution of Planetariums, Orreries and Astronomical Clocks* (Toronto, Toronto University Press; and Bristol, Adam Hilger, 1979)

Kisch, Bruno, *Scales & Weights: A Historical Outline* (New Haven, Conn., Yale University Press, 1965)

Loske, L. M., *Die Sonnenuhren: Kunstwerke der Zeitmessung und Ihre Geheimnisse* (Berlin, Springer-verlag, 1959)

Maistrov, L. E., *Pribory i instrumenty istoricheskogo znacheniya: Nauchnyi pribory* [Apparatus and instruments of historical importance: Scientific apparatus] (Moscow, Nauka, 1968)

Michel, Henri, *Scientific Instruments in Art and History* (London, Barrie & Rockliff, 1967 [also published in French and German])

Middleton, W. E. Knowles, *Catalog of Meteorological Instruments in the Museum of History and Technology* (Washington, D.C., Smithsonian Institution Press, 1969)

Nachet, *Maison Nachet: Catalogues de Fonds de 1854 à 1910* (with Introduction by G. L'E. Turner, Paris, Editions Alain Brieux, 1979)

National Maritime Museum, *The Planispheric Astrolabe* (London, HMSO, 1976)

Pullan, J. M., *The History of the Abacus* (London, Hutchinson, 1969)

Purtle, Helen R., editor, *The Billings Microscope Collection of the Medical Museum Armed Forces Institute of Pathology* (Washington, D.C., American Registry of Pathology, 1967)

Randier, Jean, *Nautical Antiques for the Collector* (English translation, London, Barrie and Jenkins, 1976)

Richeson, A. W., *English Land Measuring to 1800: Instruments and Practice* (Cambridge, Mass., MIT Press, 1966)

Rooseboom, Maria, *Bijdrage tot de Geschiedenis der Instrumentmakerskunst in de Noordelijke Nederlanden tot omstreeks 1840* (Leyden, Rijksmuseum voor de Geschiedenis der Natuurwetenschappen, 1950)

Savage, George, *The Art and Antique Restorers' Handbook: A Dictionary of Materials and Processes used in the Restoration and Preservation of all kinds of Works of Art* (London, Barrie and Jenkins, revised edn., 1976)

Skopec, Rudolf, *Photographie im Wandel der Zeiten* (Amsterdam, Letteren and Kunst, 1964)

Taylor, E. G. R., *The Mathematical Practitioners of Tudor and Stuart England* (Cambridge, Cambridge University Press, 1954)

Taylor, E. G. R., *The Mathematical Practitioners of Hanoverian England 1714-1840* (Cambridge, Cambridge University Press, 1966)

Taylor, E. G. R., *The Haven-Finding Art: a History of Navigation from Odysseus to Captain Cook* (London, Hollis and Carter, revised edn., 1971)

Thomas, D. B. *The Science Museum Photography Collection* (London, HMSO, 1969)

Turner, G. L'E., and Levere, T. H., *Van Marum's Scientific Instruments in Teyler's Museum*, Martinus van Marum: Life and Work, IV (Leyden, Noordhoff International Publishing, 1973)

Turner, G. L'E., *Essays on the History of the Microscope* (Oxford, Senecio Publishing Co. Ltd, 1979)

Turner, Gerard L'E., *Collecting Microscopes* (London, Studio Vista, 1980)

Waters, David W., *The Art of Navigation in England in Elizabethan and Early Stuart Times* (London, Hollis and Carter, 1958; reprinted, 1979)

Wheatland, David P., *The Apparatus of Science at Harvard, 1765-1800* (Cambridge, Mass., Harvard University Press, 1968)

Wynter, Harriet, and Turner, Anthony, *Scientific Instruments* (London, Studio Vista, 1975)

Zevenboom, K. M. C., and Koning, D. A. Wittop *Nederlandse Gewichten, Stetsels, Ijkwezen, Vormen, Makers en Merken* (2nd edn., Amsterdam, N.V. Uitgeversmij De Tijdstroom, 1970)

Zinner, Ernst, *Deutsche und Niederländsche Astronomischen Instrumente des 11-18 Jahrhunderts* (Munich, 1956)

Museums and Collections

A comprehensive guide to world museums is *The Directory of Museums* by Kenneth Hudson and Ann Nicholls, pub. Macmillan, London, 1975. An essential guide to Britain is *Museums & Galleries in Great Britain & Ireland*, issued annually by ABC Historic Publications, Dunstable, Bedfordshire. For West Germany, there is the well-illustrated, 800-page book edited by Klemens Mörmann, *Der deutsche Museums Führer in Farbe*, pub. Wolfgang Krüger Verlag, Frankfurt-am-Main, 1979.

Belgium
Museum of the History of Science, Korte Meer 9, Ghent

Czechoslovakia
National Technical Museum, Kostelni 42, Prague

France
Conservatoire des Arts et Métiers, 292 rue Saint-Martin, 75016 Paris
Musée de l'Observatoire, 61 avenue de l'Observatoire, 75014 Paris

GDR (East Germany)
Staatlischer Mathematisch-Physikalischer Salon im Zwinger, Dresden 801

GFR (West Germany)
Hessisches Landesmuseum, Brüder Grimm Platz 5, 3500 Kassel 1
Deutsches Museum, Museumsinsel 1, 8000 Munich 22

Great Britain
Whipple Museum of the History of Science, Free School Lane, Cambridge CB2 3RH
National Maritime Museum, Greenwich, London SE10 9NF
The Science Museum, South Kensington, London SW7 2DD
North Western Museum of Science and Industry, 97 Grosvenor Street, Manchester M1 7HF
Museum of the History of Science, Broad Street, Oxford OX1 3AZ
The Royal Scottish Museum, Chambers Street, Edinburgh EH1 1JF

India
Birla Industrial and Technological Museum, 19A Gurusaday Road, Calcutta 700019

Ireland
Egestorff Collection, 25 Wellington Place, Dublin 4

Italy
Museo di Storia della Scienza, Piazza dei Giudici 1, 50122 Florence

Netherlands
Teyler's Museum, Spaarne 16, Haarlem
Museum Boerhaave, Steenstraat 1a, 2312 BS Leyden
Utrechts Universiteits Museum, Trans 8, Utrecht

Sweden
Tekniska Museet, Museivägen 7, 115 27 Stockholm

Switzerland
Musée de l'Histoire des Sciences, 128 rue de Lausanne, Geneva

USSR ·
M. V. Lomonosov Museum, Universitetskaya Nab., Leningrad
Polytechnic Museum, 3 Novaya Ploshad, Moscow

USA
Adler Planetarium, 1300 S. Lake Shore Drive, Chicago, Illinois 60605
National Museum of History and Technology, Smithsonian Institution, Washington, D.C. 20560